W9-ARX-097

Alpha
Teach Yourself

American Sign Language

ALPHA

A member of Penguin
Group (USA) Inc.

in **24**
hours

Alpha Teach Yourself American Sign Language in 24 Hours

International Standard Book Number: 1-59257-130-1
Library of Congress Catalog Card Number: 2003111795

Printed in the United States of America

First printing: 2003

12   11   15 14 13 12 11

Note: This publication contains the opinions and ideas of its author. It is intended to provide helpful and informative material on the subject matter covered. It is sold with the understanding that the author and publisher are not engaged in rendering professional services in the book. If the reader requires personal assistance or advice, a competent professional should be consulted.

The author and publisher specifically disclaim any responsibility for any liability, loss or risk, personal or otherwise, which is incurred as a consequence, directly or indirectly, of the use and application of any of the contents of this book.

Trademarks

All terms mentioned in this book that are known to be or are suspected of being trademarks or service marks have been appropriately capitalized. Alpha Books and Penguin Group (USA) Inc. cannot attest to the accuracy of this information. Use of a term in this book should not be regarded as affecting the validity of any trademark or service mark.

Most Alpha books are available at special quantity discounts for bulk purchases for sales promotions, premiums, fund-raising, or educational use. Special books, or book excerpts, can also be created to fit specific needs.

For details, write: Special Markets, Alpha Books, 375 Hudson Street, New York, NY 10014.

PUBLISHER
Marie Butler-Knight

PRODUCT MANAGER
Phil Kitchel

SENIOR MANAGING EDITOR
Jennifer Chisholm

SENIOR ACQUISITIONS EDITOR
Mike Sanders

DEVELOPMENT EDITOR
Michael Koch

PRODUCTION EDITOR
Billy Fields

COPY EDITOR
Molly Schaller

COVER DESIGNERS
Charis Santillie
Douglas Wilkins

BOOK DESIGNER
Gary Adair

INDEXER
Tonya Heard

LAYOUT/PROOFREADING
Angela Calvert
John Etchison
Becky Harmon

TECHNICAL EDITOR
Edna Johnston

PHOTO CREDITS
Randy Shank

This book is dedicated to Lewis L. Suggs, who gave me ASL, and to Anita Kroll, who gave me life.

Overview

Contents

Introduction

American Sign Language has been said to be the third-most used language in America, after English and Spanish. People have been flocking to community centers and colleges to learn ASL, and ASL books have been flying off the shelves. ASL seems like a fun, fascinating language to learn—and it is.

You would be hard-pressed to know how to throw a javelin or how to build a house simply by reading a book. It's quite difficult—dare we say impossible—to learn ASL from reading a book alone. But fear not; you haven't wasted your money on this book.

This book should be used as a tool for your learning of the language rather than as a singular method of learning ASL. There are several ideal ways to learn the language, such as taking a course or learning it from a deaf person; learning it *only* from a book is not practical.

It has been said that for an ASL beginner to become as fluent as a native signer, he or she needs total immersion in the language and Deaf community for 7 to 10 years.

ASL is a three-dimensional language. Because this book is, of course, not three-dimensional, I've taken steps to somewhat compensate for this. I've tried to present you with photographs of Deaf native signers demonstrating how to sign words, rather than using illustrations. Every individual directly involved with this book's contents is either a second- or third-generation Deaf person who has been using ASL all his or her life, or is a near-native signer. The photographed signers will demonstrate the nonmanual signals that are central to ASL and often not shown in illustrations; hopefully this will give you a clearer idea of how to sign words. But, again, there's no better way to learn sign language than from an actual ASL user.

One way to use this book is to use it as a study aid while you take a class taught by a native signer (the most ideal situation), or by a Deaf person who is fluent in ASL. There are many hearing people who are fluent in ASL who teach the language (such as children of deaf adults, or CODA). However, having a Deaf teacher who is fluent in ASL (as opposed to sign language in general) puts a unique take on learning the language, especially because he or she is a member of the Deaf community and brings the cultural aspects of the language to the class. Not all deaf people are fluent in ASL, and not all ASL teachers are fluent in the language.

Another ideal method for learning ASL is to maintain relationships with deaf people. Interacting with them, spending time with them, and observing them will help you pick up the nuances of ASL that cannot be taught by a book.

Be sure not to expect all deaf people to devote all their free time to teaching you ASL. Instead, ask your deaf friends to become tutors, working with you on a weekly basis. ASL is just like any other language; you wouldn't go to Spain and expect the Spanish natives to spend all their time talking with you, patiently teaching you the language, especially when they're among their own people. In some states, ASL tutors and mentors are trained and available to provide services at a reasonable fee. Contact your state's American Sign Language Teachers Association (ASLTA) or Registry of Interpreters for the Deaf (RID) chapter to see if such services exist.

The bottom line: Take a class *and* socialize with deaf people. There's no better way to learn ASL. Use this book, however, as a tool to serve as a refresher or as "crib notes" while you're at home practicing and learning. There are videotapes, CDs, and DVDs available that are good assets to your learning process. (Be sure to check the credentials of the people involved with these videotapes or CD/DVDs, because many people have learned ASL as a second language or teach sign language as opposed to ASL.) It is also important that you recognize that by reading this book, you will not become fluent in nor an expert on ASL.

TIPS FOR USING THIS BOOK

Here are some tips that help you make the most of this book:

- **Actually try the signs.** As you read through the book, feel free to form the signs with your hands. If you worry you'll look silly as you try the signs, do it where nobody can see you. As mentioned earlier, I've used actual photographs of native signers, rather than illustrations. If you feel unsure of any of the signs, ask your teacher or deaf friends for feedback. You also might want to use a mirror or a video camera to see if your signs match the shown signs.

- **Keep a vocabulary log.** You'll encounter a lot of words in this book. A good approach is to keep a vocabulary log with all the signs shown. You can write your own notes to help you remember the signs. I've also included a vocabulary list of signs shown at the end of each chapter when applicable.

- **Practice, practice, and practice.** Learning ASL is just like learning any other language: It takes a great deal of time, a great deal of commitment, and you must endure a great deal of frustration. It also takes a lot of practice. People who learn other spoken languages (French, for example) know it takes hours and hours, even years, of actual practice. The same is true for ASL. ASL teachers often tell their students not to miss one class, because missing one class will greatly hinder a signer's learning process. ASL is not only a language, but it's also a *physical* language that to be remembered must be used.

- **Socialize.** Attend deaf events as much as you can, and observe people sign. Be careful, though, not to stare or be rude. You will be introduced to a wide range of people, and not all of them will embrace hearing students. Observing signers in their natural environment is one of the best ways to pick up the language, but try not to interfere in the environment.

- **Get rid of all thoughts of English grammar and syntax.** This is the hardest part for a lot of ASL students. English has been the first language of most students for the majority of their lives, so their minds are naturally set in English word order. This does not work in learning ASL, and will seriously hinder the path to fluency, because ASL has its own grammar and rules that are completely separate from English.

  Some ASL students or signers will sign using ASL signs in English order. This often distinguishes the beginning signers from the fluent ones. You will not achieve fluency in ASL until you achieve a total disregard of English rules. And that's easier said than done!

- **Enjoy the learning process.** You will get frustrated, embarrassed, flustered, and dismayed at times during the ASL learning process. That's perfectly fine—it's a new language, new experience, and new culture. The most important thing is to *enjoy* the learning process, and as you learn about the new community, have fun.

Last but not least, this book has miscellaneous tips, shortcuts, and warning sidebar boxes. Here's how they stack up:

 FYI sidebars offer advice, provide additional information, or teach an easier way to do something.

STRICTLY DEFINED

Strictly Defined boxes offer definitions of words you might not know.

PROCEED WITH CAUTION

Proceed with Caution boxes are warnings. They warn you about potential problems and help you steer clear of trouble.

Without much more ado, let's get started on your journey into this wonderful community and its language!

About the Author

Trudy Suggs, born Deaf to Deaf parents, grew up with ASL as her first language. She graduated from Gallaudet University with a B.A. in Communication Arts and Government, and earned an M.P.A. in Public Administration from the University of Illinois–Chicago. Suggs, who has her ASLTA certification, has worked as an ASL instructor, nonprofit administrator, and editor in chief of a national deaf community newspaper. In addition to teaching nonfiction writing, Trudy is a full-time writer and editor. She makes her home in Minnesota.

Acknowledgments

Eternal gratitude must be offered to the people involved with this book: Edna Johnston, my walking ASL library, and Pam Clohesey and Willie Smith, the signers who endured sweltering hours in front of the camera.

People who were unwavering in their belief in me also must be eternally thanked: Russ Conte for leading me to this book; Steve Baldwin for his ever-quirky and brilliant perspectives; Mike Kaika for his constant quips; Alejo Rodriguez for providing inspiration; Maisha Franklin, my YES! friend; Anita and Kent Kroll for their room and board and dog-sitting services; Marjorie McMullen for her wisdom; and Malcolm and Isre for their patience and loyalty.

But the deepest appreciation I can offer must go to Randy Shank: friend, ally, partner in life, and the one who always encouraged me beyond self-imposed limits.

PART I
Overview

PART 1

Overview

HOUR 1

Taking a Look at the History of ASL

LESSON PLAN:

In this hour, you'll learn about ...

- How ASL became standardized.
- The history of residential schools.
- Why ASL was banned in schools.
- Educational options for deaf students.
- How ASL is perceived today.

Chances are you've seen someone use sign language somewhere. Maybe you saw someone at a restaurant signing, or perhaps you saw Linda Bove on *Sesame Street,* or Oscar winner Marlee Matlin in a movie. American Sign Language (ASL) is believed to be the third most widely used language (after English and Spanish) in the United States today; deaf people are finding that waiters, sales associates, and other individuals know some signs. It's not surprising if you became interested in sign language after seeing someone use ASL, and found the language fascinating to watch.

ASL hasn't had an easy journey, though. The path to being recognized as a language has been long and difficult, and the history of ASL must be understood to appreciate the language. Even though sign language has been used around the world for centuries, only within the past 40 years has ASL been researched and recognized as a stand-alone, actual language.

THE HISTORY OF ASL

Deaf Americans and Canadians certainly used sign language before it became standardized in American schools. However, there were no schools or gatherings in which deaf people had a chance to congregate and share sign language. Deaf people, often isolated from each other, were left to devise their own methods of communicating with hearing friends and family.

There appears to have been no standardized sign language in the country until the early 1800s, when the first deaf residential school was founded in 1817. During the years before, deaf people used invented signs or gestures to communicate with each other in their immediate areas, and with their families. These basic communication systems are still used today, especially if the deaf person has a hearing family who has not learned sign language.

THE STANDARDIZATION OF ASL

The story of how ASL came to be standardized is a story of struggles and exploration. In 1814, a brilliant hearing man named Thomas Hopkins Gallaudet, who had entered Yale University at the age of 14, was studying to become a minister in Hartford, Connecticut, when he met a little deaf girl. Alice Cogswell was the nine-year-old daughter of Gallaudet's neighbor, Dr. Mason Cogswell. Gallaudet spent time with Alice and tried to teach her written English and the finger-spelled alphabet while developing an interest in deaf education. Dr. Cogswell then asked Gallaudet to begin efforts in founding a school for deaf students. After raising funds, Gallaudet was sent to Europe to study methods of instruction for deaf people with the hopes of bringing the methods to America.

While in Great Britain, Gallaudet visited the Braidwood Institute in England, where the oral method was used for instruction. Frustrated by Braidwood's refusal to provide him with specific instructional methods but impressed by a presentation given in London by visiting French teachers, Gallaudet decided to visit their deaf school in Paris.

STRICTLY DEFINED

The **oral method** is a method of communication where only the spoken word and lipreading or speechreading (which is the more appropriate term to use) are used with deaf students. Teachers do not sign, and students are expected to speak orally as well. Speech therapy is emphasized, often more so than language training.

In Paris, Gallaudet observed the methods of the deaf French teachers. The teachers, abbé Sicard, Laurent Clerc, and Jean Massieu, used a bilingual approach developed by abbé de l'Epée, with an emphasis on using French Sign Language to teach French and other subjects. Gallaudet witnessed firsthand the success of their unique signed approach among the deaf students, and asked to be taught their instructional methods. Meanwhile, as he learned their methods, Gallaudet learned LSF (an acronym for French Sign Language), which had an impact upon the development of ASL.

After a few years, Gallaudet brought Clerc, who was only 30 years old, back to America. In 1817, they established the Connecticut Asylum for the Education and Instruction of Deaf and Dumb Persons (later renamed American School for the Deaf) in Hartford. American was the first official school in America for deaf students, and was an asset in the standardization of the various forms of sign language found among students. With the students centralized in one location, it became possible to integrate all the various home signs and French Sign Language into what is now American Sign Language. ASL, to this day, continues to have a strong French influence on its signs.

FYI Many schools formerly used the words "Deaf and Dumb" in their names. In the old days, "dumb" meant to be mute or unable to speak. The word is occasionally used today, but it is looked upon with offense by deaf people. Mute and hearing-impaired are also generally not accepted by deaf people. Rather, the appropriate term is "deaf."

THE FIRST SCHOOLS FOR DEAF STUDENTS

With the growth of residential school education in America bringing the total number of schools to six in 1843, deaf people of all ages were flocking to residential schools for education. And it was during this time, when secondary education and postsecondary education was rare for any person, that the idea of forming a college for deaf students was conceived. The chronology and details of the formation of a college are outlined in *History of the College for the Deaf: 1857–1907*, written by Edward Miner Gallaudet, Thomas H. Gallaudet's hearing son.

Edward was a prodigy like his father. At the age of 19, he was hired as the superintendent of the Columbia Institution of the Deaf and Dumb and Blind in 1857, with his deaf mother, Sophia Fowler Gallaudet, as the school's first matron. It is interesting to note that Sophia was one of the first students at the American School for the Deaf under Laurent Clerc's tutelage.

In 1864, President Abraham Lincoln signed the charter that officially changed the school's name to Gallaudet College, named after Thomas Hopkins Gallaudet. Today the school, now Gallaudet University, continues to be the world's only liberal arts college for deaf and hard of hearing students. It wasn't until 1988 that a deaf president was appointed to the university, after a well-publicized student-led protest when a hearing president and the college's first woman president was hired over two qualified deaf candidates. Elisabeth Zinser was the only candidate who did not know sign language and had no prior experience with deaf people.

Students, alumni, and faculty, deaf and hearing alike, were outraged when they discovered that Jane Spilman, the Gallaudet Board of Trustees Chair, said during a press conference that deaf people were "not ready to function in a hearing world." She later denied having made the comment, but students burned effigies of Spilman, anyway. The fact that she had never learned sign language in all her years of being Chair also didn't go over well with the protestors and only served to support their feelings that their needs were not being understood or met by the university.

Students and alumni revolted by shutting down the campus for a week, and making four demands: Zinser would have to resign and a deaf president be appointed; the chairperson of the Board of Trustees, Jane Spilman, would also have to resign; the Board would have a 51 percent majority of deaf members; and there would be no reprisals against students or employees. I. King Jordan, who became late-deafened from a motorcycle accident at the age of 21, was selected the new president, and Phil Bravin, a deaf man with deaf children, was elected Chair of the Board of Trustees. The protest, which generated international media attention, was a *major* milestone in deaf history: 124 years after a college for deaf students was established, the student body finally had one of its own as president—but not without struggle.

THE ROLE OF EDUCATION

Traditional hearing-oriented education has always been, and continues to be, a thorn in the use of ASL.

The answer to why schools have long prevented the use of American Sign Language might be the same reason that caused so many setbacks during the late 1800s: hearing people's refusal to accept sign language as a successful instructional method. First, let's go back to 1880, when the International Congress of Instructors for the Deaf was held in Milan, Italy.

A BAN ON SIGN LANGUAGE

It was at the International Congress of Instructors for the Deaf that 1 deaf and 163 hearing educators voted to ban sign language from all education of the deaf. They felt that using sign language provided the deaf children with a crutch, giving them a reason for not learning how to speak—which, to them, was essential to living a normal life. Edward Miner Gallaudet wrote in his book, "I wish, however, to say that, by promoters of the oral method of instructing the deaf to the exclusion of the manual [language], the action of the Milan Congress in approving this policy has been unjustly taken as of the greatest possible weight in deciding upon the real merits of respective methods."

Gallaudet also noted that only 21 of the 164 delegates came from countries other than Italy and France. This is an interesting fact, because during the conference, Italy demonstrated the success of the oral method by using deaf children. Gallaudet and other opponents of the oral method noticed that the children responded to the questions asked of them *before* the questions had even been asked—proof that the demonstration was rehearsed and the children had memorized their lines.

FYI According to Barry Crouch and John Van Cleve, authors of *A Place of Their Own*, the actual proposal that banned sign language was as follows:

The Convention, considering the incontestable superiority of speech over signs, (1) for restoring deaf-mutes to social life, and (2) for giving them greater facility of language, declares that the method of articulation should have the preference over that of signs in the instruction and education of the deaf and dumb.

The vote was almost unanimous. Only six people voted against it, and five of the dissenters were Americans. "The presiding officer Dr. Lachariere, who had been the attending physician of the Paris Institution, was a bitter and unscrupulous oralist, making several most unjust rulings which treated me very unfairly," Gallaudet wrote. "The officers of the Paris Institution felt themselves so much aggrieved by the placing of Dr. Lachariere in charge of the Congress that none of them would attend its sessions. Had I known about this state of affairs in advance, I do not think I should have taken any part in the Congress." (Gallaudet, 197)

One of the renowned proponents of the oral approach, and a foe of Edward Gallaudet, was telephone inventor Alexander Graham Bell. Bell was one of the attendees at the Milan conference who voted in favor of banning sign language from schools. He also was a great supporter of eugenics, a science that deals with the improvement, through mating, of hereditary qualities of a race or breed. In layman's terms: Bell was against the idea of deaf people marrying other deaf people, and in favor of selective breeding. Imagine what he would say today if he knew that 90 to 93 percent of deaf children come from hearing parents!

FYI A. G. Bell was a fluent, experienced signer whose mother was hard of hearing. Bell also married a student he had formerly tutored, a nonsigning deaf woman. It is believed he married her for her wealth, because she was from a prominent family.

EFFECTS OF THE BAN

After the ban on the use of sign language in schools went into effect, deaf students struggled in educational institutions for nearly a century. Many will tell you stories of being hit with rulers on their hands or given other forms of punishment when they were caught using sign language. Many of those students struggled to communicate when using only the oral approach, especially those who had never been taught speech.

Even with the ban, the use of sign language persisted. Students signed during recess, often in secret, and out of the sight of educators or dormitory resident advisors. Deaf people continued to use ASL with deaf children—especially with children who had deaf parents. ASL was also almost always the language of choice at deaf gatherings.

With hearing educators forcing their opinions upon deaf people and the education of deaf people in these days, it's amazing that ASL was able to survive and flourish. Even today, hearing educators continue to underestimate the importance of allowing deaf students to use what is usually their natural, true language: American Sign Language. Schools continue to offer ASL classes that are for hearing students rather than deaf students; and there is no existent curriculum designated for education in ASL alone.

Perhaps deaf leader George Veditz, a staunch supporter of ASL, said it best when in 1913 he said, "As long as we have Deaf people, we will have sign language." The rare film footage of his signed declaration is at the Gallaudet University Archives in Washington, D.C.

EDUCATION TODAY

Today, most residential schools have returned to the use of sign language, although there are still a few oral schools in existence, such as the Clarke School in Northampton, Massachusetts, and the Central Institute for the Deaf in St. Louis, Missouri. The return to the use of sign language in the classroom did not come about until the 1970s, which shows the large impact the Milan conference had on ASL and deaf education. Most schools still offer speech therapy, and there are day programs for deaf children that use the oral approach only.

Deaf education has come a long way, and there is a wide variety of educational options for deaf children. Let's take a look at some of them:

- **Mainstreaming** Also called *inclusion*. Deaf students are placed in "regular" classes among hearing students, sometimes with interpreters and support services. In many instances, the deaf student is the only one in the entire school who is deaf. See Day programs at the end of this list.

- **Charter schools** Day schools which often are located in larger cities; these include the Metro Deaf School in St. Paul, Minnesota, and Rocky Mountain Deaf School in Lakewood, Colorado. Charter schools often use the bilingual approach, using ASL and written English to teach deaf students, and often have high success rates. Some charter schools use the oral method of teaching. These schools started appearing during the 1990s, mainly as an alternative to existent educational options for deaf students.

- **Residential schools** Students have the choice of being day students or living in dormitories. In residential schools, the students are all deaf, and the teachers, administrators, and staff are deaf or hearing. Some residential schools use the oral method, but the term "residential school" often implies the school's use of sign language. Residential schools are a strong part of Deaf culture, because the shared experiences bring deaf students together both during their childhoods and adult lives.

- **Day programs** Also called self-contained classes. Students attend programs available specifically for deaf students that are usually located at public schools. These programs often have teachers trained in instruction of the deaf, along with the choice of mainstreaming with support services.

Deaf students wishing to pursue postsecondary education supposedly have almost no limitations on their choices. With the Americans with Disabilities Act, the Rehabilitation Act of 1973, and other pertinent laws, they are afforded equal access (in theory) at universities and colleges across the nation.

Gallaudet University continues to be a popular choice for deaf students, and there are several other college programs for deaf students such as the National Technical Institute for the Deaf at the Rochester Institute of Technology in Rochester, New York, and California State University, Northridge. There is a long list of deaf people who have earned their doctorates from universities all over the world.

However, it is a sad fact that many residential schools, an important part of the deaf community, are in danger of closing down. Some even have already been shut permanently, such as the Nebraska School for the Deaf and the

Wyoming School for the Deaf. Other schools have seen dwindling numbers and cuts in state funding.

Why is this? Where are the deaf students? Is there a decline in the numbers of deaf children? There are a number of possible reasons, mainly stemming from difference of opinions and lack of awareness.

Some parents resist the idea of sending their deaf children to a residential school because they equate it with "institutionalizing" their children, or feel the educational levels at the deaf schools are not of quality. They think the residential experience is often traumatizing, when the opposite is often true for deaf students. Deaf adults often remember their years at deaf schools fondly, because it usually was the only place where they were given full communication access to teachers, friends, extracurricular activities, and daily activities.

Parents might also feel uncomfortable that deaf children might learn a new language that they are not fluent at or do not know, and might be afraid that their children will never learn the English language (or how to speak it). It's only natural that parents want their children to have their values, norms, and language. However, research has shown that teaching children English as a second language, with ASL being the first language, has proven to be successful. Most of the failures stem from having been educated by nonfluent signers who cannot understand the students or express themselves at a level that the students can understand. We explore this more in Hour 3.

Deaf children with deaf parents, as well as hearing children with deaf parents (known as CODA), often have superior language skills in both ASL and English, in addition to having above-average social skills and world knowledge. In fact, four student leaders, who were all deaf with deaf parents, led the Deaf President Now protest at Gallaudet in 1988. Many of the authors on books relating to deafness, superintendents of schools, and leaders within the Deaf community are people—either deaf or hearing—who have deaf parents.

STRICTLY DEFINED

CODA stands for child of deaf adults. This term refers to hearing children born to deaf parents. Often bilingual and bicultural, CODA have a strong community and have their own organization at www.coda-international.org.

Another possible reason is that many doctors and audiologists do not always tell parents of available educational and communication options, and parents are unaware of all available options. Doctors and audiologists often suggest that parents use the oral approach to communicate with their deaf children, but these professionals often do not provide the wide range of communication choices that are available, and rarely do the "professional experts" refer these parents to deaf, ASL-using adults who are successful and productive citizens. Parents who have hopes that deaf children will lead "normal" lives trust these doctors and audiologists, especially because they are the supposed experts. Often, parents do not realize the full range of options they have until much later.

Keep in mind that opinions are also divided among deaf and hard of hearing people. There are many success stories of deaf people who were raised using the oral approach and choose not to use sign language, such as Miss America 1995, Heather Whitestone. Even so, the rate of success of those who were educated using the oral method is very low. Attitudes toward oral education within the Deaf community might often be negative, as is written in *Deaf Heritage* by Jack R. Gannon:

> This attempt to make a "hearing" person out of a deaf child; to demand that the child talk, talk, talk and to forbid him or her the use of that natural means of communication, to refuse to permit him or her to relate to other members of the deaf community are seen by many deaf people as cruel, unrealistic and unfair. People who do this would never think of giving a blind child a pair of glasses and demanding that the child see, see, see. Nor would they be so hardhearted as to take away the crutches from a crippled child. Yet in their determination to make a deaf child "normal," these same people unconsciously deny the deaf child the right to be himself. They are, in effect, saying that it is wrong to be deaf. (Gannon, 360)

However, there are many supporters of the oral method, including those who were educated orally, who disagree with this perspective. There are certainly well-informed parents who *do* choose the oral approach. Whatever choices the parents make, one thing is for sure: Communication that begins at an early age—especially communication that the child feels comfortable with—is essential to language development.

The sign language method versus the oral method debate continues to this day. What we *do* know is that research proves American Sign Language is a real language with its own grammatical rules, syntax, and vocabulary. It is the only language out of all the possible communication systems, and does not hinder a deaf person's ability to learn English if taught at an early age. Thanks to success stories, research, and awareness, the use of ASL in schools is more accepted. High schools and colleges are now offering foreign language credit for ASL courses, which has certainly helped the growth of deaf awareness and respect for ASL. Even so, the journey is long from over.

HOUR'S UP

Here's a quiz to help you review some of the facts and ideas presented during this hour. Some of the questions have more than one answer. (You can find the correct answers in Appendix A.)

1. American Sign Language has its roots in …

   a. British Sign Language.

   b. French Sign Language.

   c. Swedish Sign Language.

   d. Home signs.

2. The first residential school for deaf students was founded in 1817 in …

   a. Hartford, Connecticut.

   b. Washington, D.C.

   c. Philadelphia, Pennsylvania.

   d. Baltimore, Maryland.

3. The 1880 conference in Milan was a setback to ASL because …

   a. It outlawed the use of oral instruction in educating deaf students.

   b. Deaf people were forbidden from teaching.

   c. It outlawed the use of ASL in educating deaf students.

   d. Deaf students were not allowed to attend school.

4. Alexander Graham Bell believed that …

   a. Deaf people should breed only with each other and remain contained.

   b. Deaf people should not breed with each other.

   c. The oral method was the only acceptable method to instruct deaf people.

   d. ASL was a successful method to use in instructing deaf people.

5. How many deaf people have deaf parents?

   a. 54 to 60 percent

   b. 30 to 35 percent

   c. 7 to 10 percent

   d. 20 to 24 percent

6. The most common educational method for deaf students today is …
   a. Residential schools
   b. Mainstreaming
   c. Oral schools
   d. Charter schools

7. True or False: The only liberal arts college for deaf students in the world is the National Technical Institute for the Deaf in Rochester, New York.

8. Research shows that children, hearing or deaf, who learn American Sign Language as a first language usually …
   a. Are delayed in speech and language development.
   b. Struggle with education.
   c. Are equal or superior to their peers in language and social development.
   d. Are excellent leaders and students.

9. Parents with newly diagnosed deaf children are likely to trust the advice of …
   a. Audiologists and doctors.
   b. Deaf people.
   c. Teachers.
   d. Other parents.

10. True or False: American Sign Language is a language separate from any other language, and has its own grammar, syntax, and vocabulary.

RECAP

This hour covered the history of American Sign Language and the deaf community's struggles in using ASL and being given fair opportunity at education. You also learned why hearing people often are resistant to the use of ASL, how beneficial ASL is to deaf and hearing people; and the risks a parent might face about a deaf child's communication methods. In the next hour, you'll study Deaf culture and its relationship to ASL and the community.

HOUR 2

Understanding Deaf Culture

LESSON PLAN:

In this hour, you'll learn about ...

- The definition of Deaf culture.
- Aspects of Deaf culture.
- Values of Deaf culture.
- Causes of hearing loss.
- Common myths about deaf people.
- Technological influences.
- Paradigms of the Deaf community.

There are 26 million deaf and hard of hearing people in America, but only a very small percentage of these people identify themselves as being members of the culturally Deaf community. Culturally Deaf people use ASL to communicate and congregate with other culturally Deaf people. It's essential that ASL students understand what Deaf culture is in order to fully understand the role of ASL within the deaf community.

WHAT IS DEAF CULTURE?

Although there are many definitions of what Deaf culture is, perhaps Dr. Barbara Kannapell, a deaf professor at Gallaudet University, says it best when she observes that Deaf culture is "a set of learned behaviors and perceptions that shape the values and norms of deaf people based on their shared or common experiences."

Not every deaf and hard of hearing person is part of the culturally Deaf community. People can also be part of the deaf community without being culturally Deaf, such as interpreters or children of deaf adults (CODA). However, most people who are culturally Deaf are ASL users.

A capital D in the word Deaf usually signifies that the deaf person is culturally Deaf and uses ASL.

According to Dr. Kannapell, there are five basic aspects of Deaf culture: communication, language, perceptions, community, and sharing.

- **Communication**   Deaf people rely upon their eyes and hands to communicate, and this leads to the use of ASL, the language they use to communicate, socialize, and express ideas and thoughts. ASL is unique in that it relies on visual and hand components rather than vocal and aural components.
- **Language**   ASL is at the crux of Deaf culture.
- **Perceptions**   Deaf people's views of the world might surprise many people. Culturally Deaf people often will not choose to regain their hearing, even if given the opportunity. This surprises hearing people, especially the medical profession, because being deaf is generally considered a disability by these people. We'll explore this more later on in this hour.
- **Community**   Deaf people develop a special bond with each other, much like other minorities, because of their shared identities and experiences. This common bond then creates an exclusive community within the larger population. Among each other, Deaf people have high self-esteem, positive self-images, and confidence in themselves as a whole.

  Deaf people often will gather at deaf events (clubs for deaf people, sporting events, open-captioned films, performances, and other events) and feel a sense of belonging. Many organizations are run by and for deaf people: churches, schools, and of course, colleges and college programs.
- **Sharing**   ASL is passed down from generation to generation through several ways. Deaf families, deaf schools, and deaf gatherings are some of the ways that deaf people learn ASL. It is through this sharing that folklore, stories, literature, and history about the Deaf community is developed and preserved.

Deaf people often look upon themselves as a cultural, rather than disabled, group. In fact, they are the only "disabled" group with its own language, which might clarify why deaf people tend to consider themselves as a linguistic entity rather than a group of disabled individuals. This is another reason deaf people bristle at the term "hearing impaired," which signifies that a deaf person is broken or impaired.

THE VALUES OF DEAF CULTURE

As is true for any other culture, there are values that are cherished by Deaf people. These values, if removed, create a sense of loss. Some values include ...

- Eyes
- Hands
- Visual access
- Schools for deaf people
- Clubs for deaf people
- Sporting events
- Gatherings of deaf people

Although these are only a few of many, the common thread is clear—they all involve the use of ASL in one way or another. Schools, clubs, and events are where deaf people know there is a guarantee of communication access, as opposed to the hearing world, where the majority of people have never met a deaf person before, much less seen ASL in use.

It is interesting to note that Deaf-Blind people—people who are both deaf and blind—place importance on similar values. Dr. Oliver Sacks, psychologist and author, studied the Deaf-Blind community in a 1998 PBS television special, *Oliver Sacks: The Mind Traveller*. He participated in a Deaf-Blind summer camp in Seattle, Washington, and at a dinner, asked the Deaf-Blind people in attendance whether they'd prefer to regain their hearing or vision. Almost all said they wouldn't want to be able to hear, and would choose vision over hearing.

The lack of desire to regain hearing is a common sentiment among Deaf people, even those who are not Deaf-Blind, and might seem bizarre to hearing people. But remember: Many Deaf people do not look at their hearing loss as a lack of a sense, but rather, an enhancement of their lives that allows them access to a rich culture and language.

CAUSES OF HEARING LOSS

Before we explore the technology in a deaf person's life and the paradigms of the deaf community, let's take a quick look at the causes and types of hearing losses.

There are many causes of hearing losses. Childhood diseases, such as rubella (which created one of the biggest outbreaks of deafness during the 1960s), are among the most common causes. Hearing loss can also be drug-induced or caused by spinal meningitis, measles, genetics, and age. Some deaf people also have tinnitus (a constant ringing or buzzing in the ear) and balance problems (especially those who became deaf from meningitis).

The age at the time of hearing loss and the type of hearing loss often play a big role in determining a deaf person's future. People who lose hearing at a later time in their lives (usually adulthood) often do not consider themselves part of the deaf community, especially if they do not learn ASL. Even so, there is a group, the Association of Late-Deafened Adults (www.alda.org), which promotes awareness and focus on the needs of late-deafened individuals. There is also the Self-Help for Hard of Hearing organization (www.shhh.org), which focuses on the needs and issues facing hard of hearing people.

The majority of people who are culturally Deaf were born deaf or were prelingually deaf. Many do not learn ASL until later in life, yet others have always known ASL. The diversity within the deaf community is as great as any other community.

MYTHS ABOUT DEAF PEOPLE

There are quite a few myths about deaf people, including the following:

- **Deaf people can't hear.** Actually, it's a rarity when a deaf person cannot hear at all. Most deaf people have some residual hearing, and many enjoy music—especially if it's turned up loud!

- **All deaf people can lipread, and lipreading is an effective communication method.** Even the most experienced speechreader catches only 30 to 40 percent of what is actually said. That means the typical speechreader will catch only 10 percent at the most of what is actually said. The rest is guesswork and more guesswork. So many words look the same on the mouth: pat, mat, bat; you, clue, cute.

  Also, not all deaf people can speechread—so it's probably better if you use other methods of communicating, such as paper and pen, or using an interpreter. Or better yet—learn ASL.

- **Deaf people can't drive.** Certainly they can! In the old days, deaf people were banned from driving (and still are in many countries), but were quickly reinstated after research showed that they were and still are considered one of the safest driver groups by insurance companies. Ninety-nine percent of driving is visually based. There are deaf pilots and truck drivers, and there's even a deaf pilot association.

- **A hearing aid makes a deaf person hear more clearly.** A hearing aid does not help a deaf person hear; it amplifies sounds. But the deaf person still has to be able to distinguish between specific sounds and speech. Not all deaf people benefit from wearing hearing aids, and many choose not to wear them.
- **Deaf people are not intelligent.** This attitude is still surprisingly prevalent in today's society. The common following of the word deaf with the word dumb doesn't help, either.

Deaf people are no different from hearing people in the intelligence department. There are deaf people with average IQs, those with low IQs, and those with above-average IQs. Many deaf people have earned doctorates; some are even members of the high-IQ organization Mensa. Composer Ludwig van Beethoven was deaf (and often carried paper and pen to communicate), as were inventor Thomas Edison and Girl Scouts founder Juliette Low. A great resource on deaf individuals who have contributed much to society is *Deaf Heritage* by Jack R. Gannon.

TECHNOLOGY IN A DEAF PERSON'S LIFE

Go to any deaf person's house and you'll probably find the doorbell fitted with a flashing light, the phone fitted with a flashing light, a wake-up alarm with either a flashing light or a vibrating device, and a television with built-in closed-captioning. There's likely a two-way pager lying on a table or on the deaf person's belt, and a computer somewhere in the house.

Technology has played a major role in the shaping of today's Deaf community and cultural values. In the old days, there were no TTYs (teletypewriters, devices that deaf people use to communicate on the phone), no closed-captioning, no e-mail, and many other assistive devices that deaf people almost take for granted today. The lack of these devices formed many cultural tendencies that persist to this day.

USING THE PHONE

Before the advent of TTYs, deaf people often would rely on deaf gatherings to socialize and pick up news about friends and relatives. An 80-year-old man remembers, "We would drive 50 miles to a friend's house in the hopes that he was home. If he wasn't, we would either wait a few hours, hoping he'd come home, or leave a note with a specific date and time that we'd be back, and drive the 50 miles home." Deaf people also would often plan for prearranged visits at deaf clubs or sporting events, because they had no way of calling each other. These visits were precious and extended; it often was their only opportunity to socialize with other deaf friends independently of nonsigners.

Deaf people also had to depend upon hearing people—whether it be a neighbor, relative, or child—to make calls for them. Even a simple call to the doctor would turn into a major activity. One woman tells of how she would have to wait until her deaf husband got home from work to watch the kids, then drive 23 miles to her mother's to have her mother make a call for her. Usually, deaf people would choose to go to the stores in person and conduct business over the counter rather than go to so much trouble.

When the first TTYs—big, clunky machines that were heavy and approximately 4 feet high—were introduced in the 1960s, it took a while for the machines to catch on. By the late 1960s and early 1970s, they were commonplace, and deaf people were unburdened from having to drive long distances to visit friends, and could now chat with others who had TTYs.

However, they still weren't able to call hearing people, unless the hearing people had TTYs. It wasn't until the 1980s that TTYs (which, by now, had been reduced to the size of a bulky laptop) were semi-affordable, at prices ranging from $500 to $1,000. Still, deaf people had to rely upon interpreters or hearing friends/relatives to make calls for them, until relay services were introduced.

RELAY SERVICES

Relay services were and are a blessing to deaf people. To use relay, a person could call a number and an operator would voice everything typed by the deaf caller to the hearing caller, while typing everything that the hearing caller spoke to the TTY user. Deaf people could now make calls independently, without having to sometimes embarrassingly disclose personal information through a colleague or relative. They could order a pizza, call the doctor, the bank, as well as their own relatives.

Even so, early relay services were limited due to funding. Deaf Contact in Chicago, a volunteer-run service during the late 1980s and early 1990s, had four separate phone lines (with four separate numbers), and limited operating hours. Calls were limited to 10-minute business calls.

This was cumbersome, because first, a person had to remember the four phone numbers in order to call relay, and second, a call could not always be completed within 10 minutes. Finally, the definition of "business" was ambiguous. People still could not call for a pizza, because the volunteer operators sometimes did not define that as a "business call."

With the passage of the Americans with Disabilities Act in 1990, relay services became a 24-hour-a-day, 7-days-a-week service with specially trained operators. Today, the relay service industry is a flourishing business with thousands of Communication Assistants (CA) relaying phone calls of all types. One only needs to dial 7-1-1 to connect to relay.

There are also a multitude of different relay services: Spanish-to-English, voice carry-over (where a deaf person speaks for himself, and the CA types what the hearing person speaks), hearing carry-over (where a hearing person who cannot speak can listen to what is said, and types on a TTY), online relay using the web, and video relay services, where a person with a web cam can use ASL to communicate instead of typed English to an interpreter/CA on camera, who will then use voice to communicate with the hearing caller.

FYI TTYs are still expensive, but many states offer a Technological Equipment Distribution Program (TEDP). TEDPs distribute varying items, such as TTYs and alert systems (phone flashers, doorbells, and smoke detectors), to qualified participants at no cost.

However, a problem persists in relay calls: hang-ups. Many people unfamiliar with relay calls will hang up, thinking the calls are from telemarketers or not wanting to deal with deaf people. Relay companies have been working on providing awareness and training, even taking out billboard ads on the highway in New Jersey and airing commercials on local television.

CLOSED CAPTIONING

Another technological advance that has been a blessing for deaf people is closed captioning. Closed captioning did not start until the late 1970s, and even during these days, only specific hours and very few shows were captioned. Today, thanks to the ADA and the Federal Communications Commission, captioning rules are all encompassing and stricter.

All televisions bigger than 13 inches must have built-in captioning, and there are specific hours a network must provide closed-captioned programming.

However, the battle is long from over. Many emergency news reports are not captioned on the local news level, and captions are not always available 24 hours a day. Even so, captioning has served more than just deaf people: Bars and restaurants often use captioning in their facilities due to the high noise level of the environment; foreigners have found it useful as a English learning tool; and parents find it is a terrific tool in teaching their children—hearing and deaf—how to read.

When silent movies began to have sound, deaf people were once again left out. As Jack R. Gannon wrote in *Deaf Heritage* in 1947, a deaf Cuban residing in New York named Emerson Romero bought some films and began adding subtitles to them. However, there were problems with the process, and resources were limited. Years later during the 1950s after much work, Captioned Films for the Deaf was passed into law as a free-loan subtitled motion picture library for deaf people.

Many deaf people remember gathering at deaf clubs every Friday to watch captioned films, a rarity since the days of the silent films. With time, captioned films were phased out by captioned videotapes, and now captioned DVDs are available. The program is still in existence, although it is now called the Captioned Media Program (www.cfv.org), coordinated by the National Association of the Deaf.

FYI Charlie Chaplin, a famous silent film actor, was a great friend of the deaf community and knew how to fingerspell. Chaplin often credited his pantomime and gesture skills to a deaf friend, Granville S. Redmond, who was an artist by trade. Redmond had small bits in some of Chaplin's films. (Gannon, 136)

Movies at the theatre are often open-captioned today, but are limited to specific showings at specific theatres throughout the country. Some theatres also offer rearview captioning, which uses a plastic visorlike device that is placed into the arm of your seat, and captions appear on the visor. However, many deaf people—much like hearing people—choose to watch movies at home rather than going out.

Captioning has also been brought into the classroom and at meetings. With technology similar to that which enables live television captioning, students now can use CART (Communication Access Realtime Translation) on a laptop for classes or at meetings.

PAGERS

Another technological advance that has made an enormous impact upon the deaf community is the use of two-way pagers. The pagers, which became widespread in 2000, are mini-keyboards that have e-mail capabilities, and in some cases, TTY and faxing capabilities. With the introduction of two-way pagers, deaf people now could have their own version of the cell phone. They could email anyone from anywhere, and even use instant messaging. In fact, AAA has partnered with Wynd Communications, a pager distributor, to provide roadside assistance via pager. Now hearing people are using these pagers, too, because they're cheaper, less intrusive, and handy. But cell phone users and pager users have a common problem: being in range!

Pagers, TTYs, captioned media, faxes, online instant messaging, e-mail—what more could a deaf person ask for? Yet, a drawback of all these technological advances is that the need for deaf people to gather at deaf clubs and events is dwindling. Instead, people prefer to stay in the comforts of their own homes, communicating online or via TTY. Pagers have it made easier to share information by transmitting even news alerts immediately.

Deaf clubs, during their glory days, numbered the hundreds, each with hundreds of members. Today, there are only a few left, with dwindling memberships. Even so, deaf events are still very much a part of the deaf community, especially with trade shows, storytelling events, and sporting events. There are national sporting tournaments with deaf referees often regulating the games.

With technology being both a burden and an asset to the deaf community, it is even more imperative that ASL continues to be taught and passed from generation to generation.

PARADIGMS OF THE DEAF COMMUNITY

As mentioned earlier, there are 26 million deaf and hard of hearing Americans, but only a small fraction of them use ASL. The rest fall into various categories, and often do not use sign language. There are senior citizens who have lost their hearing due to age, and people who suddenly become deaf later in their lives (known as late-deafened adults), who continue to have English as their first and primary language. There are also people who choose other communication methods rather than ASL and do not identify themselves closely with the deaf community in terms of culture and language.

Perhaps the best way to illustrate the intricate number of differences within the deaf community would be to use Charlotte Baker and Dennis Cokely's descriptions and illustration in *American Sign Language: A Teacher's Resource Text on Grammar and Culture*:

Avenues to membership in the Deaf community.

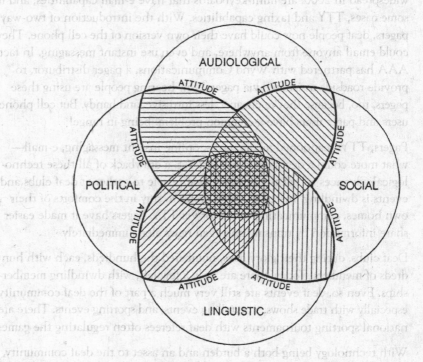

- **Audiological** Refers to actual loss of hearing ability. Thus, this avenue of membership is not available, by definition, to hearing people. It seems apparent that those individuals with a hearing loss are accepted by and identify with the Deaf community at a much deeper level ("the core") and much more quickly than a hearing person with similar skills, experience, and attitudes.
- **Political** Refers to the potential ability to exert influence on matters which directly affect the Deaf Community on a local, state, or national level. For example, a person might hold an office in a state (National Association of the Deaf) chapter. Of course, the types of decisions and proposals which he or she makes will also influence how well other members of the Deaf community accept that person.

- **Linguistic**   Refers to the ability to understand and use American Sign Language. The level of fluency seems to be related to the level of acceptance into the Deaf community. Since the values and goals of the Deaf community are transmitted by its language, it is not surprising that fluency in ASL is very important.

- **Social**   Refers to the ability to satisfactorily participate in social functions of the Deaf community. This means being invited to such functions, feeling at ease while attending, and having friends who are themselves members of the Deaf community. This ability may presuppose other factors, such as linguistic skills in ASL.

  Looking at the illustration, the core consists of people who are deaf, and very much members of the culturally Deaf community. It is possible for a person to have a hearing loss yet not be part of the Deaf community, and it is also possible for a person to have ASL knowledge—such as an interpreter—yet not be a member of the Deaf community.

A common frustration experienced by deaf people is the way some hearing people perceive the deaf community, which contrasts greatly with the way the Deaf community perceives itself. Dr. Kannapell in her as yet unpublished research lists two models, the cultural model versus the pathological model.

Two Perspectives of Deaf People

Topic	Cultural Model	Pathological Model
Intelligence	No difference	Inferior, slow learners, learning disabled
Abilities	Unlimited	Limited
Language	ASL	Speech and language are confused; language-deficient or problems
Culture	Deaf culture	Culturally deprived; isolated
Communication	Different way of communicating	Communication disorder, speech disabled
Reasoning	Full range of abilities Deaf people *can!*	Can't express abstract ideas Deaf people *can't!*

Through years of fighting, the Deaf community has preserved their language and emerged as a flourishing culture with a rich and highly complex language. Even with some values disappearing, new values are appearing in their place, and deaf people continue to fight for and value their positions within society.

HOUR'S UP!

Here's a quiz to help you review some of the facts and ideas presented during this hour. Some of the questions have more than one answer. (You can find the correct answers in Appendix A.)

1. A capital "D" in the word deaf means …
    a. The person is audiologically deaf.
    b. The person is culturally deaf.
    c. The person became deafened from disease.
    d. The person was born deaf.

2. Deaf people were finally able to make calls to hearing people independently during the …
    a. 1960s.
    b. 1970s.
    c. 1980s.
    d. 1990s.

3. The four avenues of membership in the deaf community include …
    a. Audiological, political, social, and linguistic.
    b. Audiological, social, linguistic, and cultural.
    c. Linguistic, social, cultural, and political.
    d. Audiological, social, cultural, and linguistic.

4. The Americans with Disabilities Act enabled deaf people to …
    a. Have 24-hour closed captioning.
    b. Have 24-hour relay services.
    c. Get TTYs for free anytime.
    d. Get disability benefits.

5. Deaf people gather at …
    a. School events.
    b. Sporting events.
    c. Storytelling presentations.
    d. Audiological conventions.

6. How did deaf people make phone calls in the days before the TTY?

    a. They would ask friends or relatives.

    b. They would drive to the place of business.

    c. They would resort to writing letters.

    d. They wouldn't make phone calls.

7. True or False: Every deaf person is automatically part of the culturally Deaf community.

8. The five aspects of Deaf culture are communication, language, sharing, and …

    a. Community and audiology.

    b. Perceptions and community.

    c. Perceptions and technology.

    d. Audiology and technology.

9. Deaf people look upon themselves as …

    a. Disabled.

    b. A cultural group.

    c. A linguistic entity.

    d. Impaired.

10. What is at the heart of Deaf culture?

    a. Level of hearing loss.

    b. Equality.

    c. ASL.

    d. Being able to speak.

RECAP

This hour covered the culture of deaf people and various influences on Deaf culture. With an understanding of the history of the language and the culture that revolves around ASL, you're now ready to start learning the language in the next hour.

HOUR 3
Introducing ASL

LESSON PLAN:

In this hour, you'll learn about ...

- What ASL is.
- The parameters of a sign.
- How the language has survived.
- Accents.
- Different communication methods.
- Early acquisition of the language.

According to linguists Dennis Cokely and Charlotte Baker-Shenk, ASL "is a visual-gestural language created by Deaf people .... It is also a language that is separate from any other language, with its own grammar, syntax, and vocabulary." (48)

People unfamiliar with the language often mistakenly believe it is some form of English or broken English. One reason for this might be that ASL is such a three-dimensional language that it's not possible to have a written form; but when people write down English representations of ASL signs, the grammar seems to be poorly written. In fact, the opposite is true; we'll explore grammar more in Hours 7 and 8.

A CLOSER LOOK AT ASL

ASL is unique because it has no written form, and people often assume it cannot be a language or that ASL is an English-based language. However, there are approximately 10,000 languages in the world, and only 800 have a written system. ASL is one of these 9,200 languages that exists without a written form, and is a language separate from English.

Contrary to popular belief, the language also is not a series of iconic signs—that is, a sign does not "mimic" its representation. Some signs are iconic, such as eat, tree, or sleep. However, a majority of signs are not iconic, and are highly complex formations of the hands.

Each sign consists of four parameters:

- **Handshape**   The shape of the sign.
- **Location**   Where on the body that the handshape is made. A handshape made on the chin has a different meaning from the same handshape located at the forehead.
- **Movement**   The motion of the handshape can change the word's meaning, even if the handshape and location are the same.
- **Palm orientation**   Whether the handshape/sign is facing away or toward the signer.

Let's examine the signs for *dry*, *ugly*, and *summer*. Each has the same handshape, but different locations and slightly different motions.

DRY   UGLY   SUMMER

With the four parameters and nonmanual signals, signs differ greatly from word to word. In English, one word may have multiple meanings. Using *break* as an example, you can see how a word has multiple meanings:

Let's take a break.

Our spring break is next week.

My car may break down.

Be careful or you'll break it.

There's been a break in the investigation.

In ASL, each of these definitions has a separate meaning and different sign. However, there are words in ASL that have one sign, even if they're different words with same meanings. For example, how the word *die* is signed in ASL would also be the same way for how *kicked the bucket*, *six feet under*, *passed away*, and so on are signed.

There are also signs that are compounds. For example, the word *homework* has two signs—the sign for *home* and the sign for *work*. Signs such as *daughter* and *son* are derived from the signs for *baby* and *girl/boy*. Fluent signers sign compounds in a manner that the word often seems like one sign rather than two separate signs.

FYI The sign for *home* actually evolved from two signs: *bed* and *eat*. Over time, the signs changed into one, and the sign is now the sign for *home*.

With this in mind, the student must keep in mind the concept of what is being signed, rather than try to find a literal translation.

SURVIVAL OF THE LANGUAGE

You've read about how not all deaf people use American Sign Language, and the fact that not all ASL users are deaf. You've also read about how ASL is at the core of the culturally Deaf community, and its long, difficult history. Deaf people share experiences through ASL, and this sharing of experience is what bonds them to each other. ASL is crucial to the Deaf community.

ASL has survived through oppression, removal, and attempts at redefinition. The language has survived in a number of ways, the most prevalent being through deaf people passing on ASL to other deaf people. This takes place at residential schools, programs for deaf students, and among deaf communities. For instance, a child might come to a deaf school knowing no sign at all, and learn from other students at the school, from deaf teachers, and from alumni of the school.

The other, seemingly obvious, reason ASL has survived is simple: Deaf people need it. Because Deaf people have a more visual need, they tend to prefer to use a language that is natural and requires little or no struggle (for them).

Nowadays, attempts at preserving ASL are well underway. The Archives at Gallaudet University have managed to preserve some rare footage from the embattled days of the ASL versus spoken English debate, and the staff of the Archives department also uncovered many documents about the language debate. Videotapes, DVDs, and CDs are easily available through mail-order companies for people with sparse access to the Deaf community (such as those in rural areas of the country). ASL-oriented events, such as storytelling events and performances, are widespread throughout the nation.

ACCENTS IN ASL

ASL is not a universal language. Other countries have their own sign languages, such as German Sign Language, Japanese Sign Language, and so on. Even Great Britain has its own sign language—even though both America and Great Britain use English!

Even so, often when deaf Americans travel to other countries and meet up with deaf people, they find it quite easy to communicate, because they gesture naturally, and facial expressions are quite similar in many cases. Some of the most popular gathering places for deaf people take place at the Deaflympics and World Federation for the Deaf conventions.

Within America, there are different signs from state to state, much like there are regional and local accents. A New Yorker often will sign much faster than someone from Nebraska. The word *early*, for instance, has many signed variations, and the following figures show only four of them.

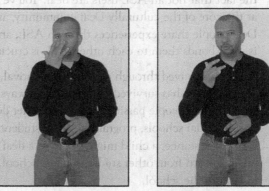

This is a commonly used version, with a finger moving across the back of the other hand.

This is used mostly by Illinois signers.

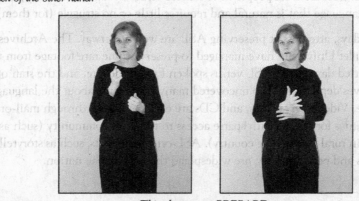

This also means PREPARE.

This sign is used mostly by Minnesota signers.

Gender is another factor in ASL "accents." Typically, accents depend on the individual, but there are certain words that tend to be signed differently by males and by females. For example, males and females might sign the word *champion* differently, although both genders may sign it either way. In the following pictures, we'll look at how the word *champion* might be signed by males and females.

She won the championship at the bowling tournament.

CHAMPION

This version is generally used by males.

CHAMPION

This version is generally used by females; the handshape can be either a bent-3 handshape or a 5 handshape.

A native signer can often identify where a person is from by his signing, and even how long he has been signing. This is akin to an English native speaker being able to identify what part of the country (or world) another person is from, and whether English is his or her first language.

COMMUNICATION METHODS

There are various communication methods other than ASL and the oral approach, although none of them are considered separate languages from English or ASL; rather, they are *communication methods*. I'll go through some of the communication modes briefly to give you a general idea.

- **Cued Speech**   Using eight handshapes in four locations around the mouth to represent spoken sounds, Cued Speech is touted as a tool for learning English. It is not a separate language.
- **Signed English**   Words are signed in English order, including tenses (*-ing*, *-ed*, *'s*, and so on). Signed English is usually is used by people who do not accept or do not feel comfortable with ASL's complex grammar and rules. It is common among hearing teachers teaching deaf people and hearing parents.
- **Contact signs**   Words are signed using a combination of ASL and Signed English. Formerly known as Pidgin Signed English.
- **Rochester method**   Rarely used today. A method where all words are fingerspelled, without any signing involved.

One important detail is that with today's rapidly changing technology, there have been the formations of some new signs, such as *fax* and *pager*. However, one cannot make up a sign simply because one wants to. The signs must gain community approval, just like English words must gain community approval.

In fact, the invention of a new sign without community approval was cause for a community uproar in 1997, when a hearing woman appeared in a Saturn car commercial. Holly Daniel, an uncertified interpreter from Louisiana, appeared in Saturn's "Real People, Real Cars" ad campaign (where actual Saturn owners were featured), and said in the advertisement she had invented a sign for *Saturn* because it was too long to fingerspell.

Deaf people watching the commercial immediately knew she was not deaf (even though Saturn and Daniel insisted she was), due to the quality of her signing and her invention of a sign that was not ASL-friendly. A reporter for a deaf community newspaper investigated and discovered that Daniel had faked her deafness for up to two years prior to the commercial. Saturn eventually pulled the TV and print campaign after the reporter wrote three articles that led to national exposure, apologizing to the Deaf community.

This is an example of how protective the Deaf community is of ASL. This is actually common among other closely-knit cultures in other parts of the world, who are wary of outsiders and protective of their cultural and linguistic norms.

EARLY ACQUISITION OF ASL

For any child, early acquisition of language is essential to personal, social, and mental growth. This is an area of risk for deaf children, especially those who have minimized communication at either home or school. The critical language acquisition period is between the ages of birth and five, according to experts, and this period is often where language learning is a serious problem for deaf children.

Many deaf children aren't diagnosed until they're at least one year old—some even much later. In these cases, the children have already gone a year or more without exposure to language, and might have tried to find other ways to compensate for the lack of language. Perhaps the deaf child tried to communicate by pointing or other natural gestures, or express through angry tactics, what he wanted. This type of behavior often results in reprimands from parents who do not want their child to behave inappropriately. This, of course, creates a Catch-22 situation: The child isn't able to express himself naturally, and the parents don't realize that this is how he expresses himself. So he then associates expressing himself with punishment.

A deaf child also might be delayed in language development, and this might follow him for the rest of his years if he is not given access to the language that is most natural to him, which in many cases, is sign language. Parents might be frightened by having to learn a whole new language, as well as frightened that their child might never be "normal" (that is, being able to speak and hear), and many choose to try and teach their children how to speak without allowing the use of sign language.

Earlier, I discussed how parents rely heavily upon the advice of audiologists and doctors. The concept of English as a Second Language (ESL) is rarely offered by these experts; instead the experts offer the options available to "fix" the deafness: intensive speech therapy, providing cochlear implants or hearing aids, and providing audiological training.

Learning how to speak with very little concept of what sound is creates a difficult learning environment. How do you show a child how to pronounce the letter K, especially if you don't have a common language with the child?

The lack of exposure to sign language to demonstrate abstract concepts or grammatical rules of English is frustrating for many deaf children, and this lack often results in poor English skills. When this occurs, people might then automatically blame sign language for the poor development of English skills, especially at residential schools or ASL-oriented programs, when the cause is actually a lack of language access rather than the use of ASL.

It is interesting to note that deaf children of deaf parents often have no problems developing English skills after having learned ASL, especially because they are given language models outside of the classroom in the form of their signing parents and other deaf people from day one.

This additional exposure to language is crucial to language development among children, hearing or deaf. Hearing children, for instance, who are speech-delayed often will pick up speech elsewhere, such as at school or in playgroups. But deaf children who come from hearing families are rarely put in situations with other deaf or signing people until later on in their lives, and are often placed in academic environments where sign language is not used. Another possible factor for delayed language development abundant in deaf education is teachers who do not sign fluently, or do not believe ASL is a language.

Some parents and teachers do not praise deaf students if they have exceptional ASL skills. Rather, parents and teachers focus heavily on the development of written and/or spoken English skills before the development of ASL. A parent of a deaf daughter says, "I would always congratulate my daughter on her voice, even if her words were mispronounced. One day, she asked me why I never congratulated her on her signs—and that's when it hit me—I was showing bias, and unintentionally preventing her language development."

FYI In 1997, a *DeafNation* newspaper reporter did a survey of 22 residential schools for deaf students in America. She found that there were no schools with a majority of deaf staff or administration, the highest being 46 percent. She concluded that because residential schools were not offering language models for deaf children, ASL could not be blamed for poor English skills. Rather, the opposite was true: A barrier to ASL was the reason so many people grew up with poor English skills.

This barrier to learning ASL, in turn, creates in many deaf people the feeling of resentment and frustration over the early years of their lives. Linguists, psychologists, and ASL experts are now recommending that hearing parents with deaf babies immerse their children in the Deaf community, meet with tutors, have deaf mentors, and even hire deaf nannies, as they pursue written and/or spoken English development.

It is ironic that although deaf people still struggle to claim ASL as a necessary educational method and language development method, researchers and educators are discovering that learning sign language is extremely beneficial to hearing babies. Dr. Marilyn Daniels at Pennsylvania State University did a study and found that children who learned sign language, both as babies and as children, scored higher on reading and aptitude tests. Her research also showed that babies are able to form gestures and babble in sign language before they can babble vocally. It will be interesting to see how her research will support the learning of ASL at an early age for deaf children.

HOUR'S UP!

Here's a quiz to help you review some of the facts and ideas presented during this hour. Some questions have more than one answer. (You can find the correct answers in Appendix A.)

1. Each sign has ___ parameters.

   a. 2
   b. 4
   c. 6
   d. 8

2. True or False: ASL is an iconic language.

3. The Rochester method of communicating is …

   a. A combination of ASL and contact signs.
   b. Mouthing every word of English.
   c. Using fingerspelling only.
   d. Similar to Braille.

4. True or False: People may make up signs to fit their needs.

5. Accents in ASL are influenced by …

   a. Gender.
   b. Location.
   c. Fluency.
   d. Intelligence.

QUIZ

6. ASL has survived mostly by …
   a. Deaf people passing the language on to other deaf people.
   b. A careful recording of signs.
   c. Hearing people passing the language on to deaf people.
   d. Deaf people passing the language on to hearing people.

7. A common communication method among nonfluent hearing signers is …
   a. The Rochester method.
   b. Cued Speech.
   c. ASL.
   d. Contact signs.

8. True or False: With changing technology, some new signs have emerged for devices such as fax machines and pagers.

9. Holly Daniel upset the Deaf community because …
   a. She claimed to be deaf and went on national television showing the invention of a sign.
   b. She was deaf and invented a sign.
   c. She was an uncertified interpreter.
   d. She got a free car.

10. Early acquisition of ASL by hearing and deaf children has proven to …
    a. Hinder a child's language development.
    b. Improve a child's language development.
    c. Be traumatic to a child's emotional development.
    d. Be beneficial for a child's emotional development.

QUIZ

RECAP

In this hour, you learned what ASL is, and you looked at how parameters influence meanings of words. You also explored how ASL has survived through centuries, considered different communication methods, and learned the importance of early acquisition of ASL. The following hour provides some conversational basics you can use when meeting deaf people.

PART II
Getting Started

HOUR 4

Conversational Basics

LESSON PLAN:

In this hour, you'll learn about ...

- Respecting boundaries within the deaf community.
- Attention-getting behaviors.
- Conversational barriers.
- Leave-taking behaviors.
- Possible scenarios.
- Good-byes.

When you start meeting deaf people, you'll encounter many situations where you're not sure what to do, or how to approach. It's imperative that, as an ASL learner, you learn the basics of conversing with a deaf person or another signer. When you learn the basics, you'll feel less of an outsider and become more comfortable in using ASL.

BEING AN OBSERVER

Robert Lee, a certified interpreter from Boston, was the keynote speaker at the 1998 Registry of Interpreters (RID) Region III conference in Chicago. He told the audience, composed mostly of interpreters and hearing people, "As a hearing, late-second-language learner of ASL, I have been invited into the lives of Deaf people, and I could just as easily be invited out. I have no intrinsic 'right' to be an interpreter, just as no outsider can claim the right to be a member of another culture, like people don't have the right to be part of a Swahili or a Native American tribe." The Deaf community has its own social norms, and because you are most likely hearing and new to the language, you will probably be considered an outsider for a while.

Don't be alarmed by this label. You can be an outsider and still learn the language and culture and even be welcomed into the community. As discussed in Hour 3, you will never be fully an insider, simply because you can hear. However, that doesn't mean you'll be rejected from the community. Quite the contrary; most of the deaf people in the community come from hearing families (remember that 90 to 93 percent statistic?), and have hearing co-workers, friends, and even spouses.

FYI Statistics claim that 85 to 90 percent of deaf people marry other deaf people. The reasons for this appear to be the same as any other culture marrying into its own culture. Both tend to have shared experiences, similar beliefs, and similar communication needs.

You can become an observer (rather than an outsider) of the community. Members of the community have grown up experiencing discrimination, oppression, and frustration—and these experiences, in turn, have brought them together into a makeshift family sharing the same experiences, language, and needs. With this in mind, if you offer respect and awareness, you'll be warmly welcomed into the community.

Your acceptance into the community also depends upon your attitude and fluency at ASL. If you bring a paternalistic attitude of "I'm here to help you," you'll most likely be ignored or rejected. Most deaf people feel they do not need help nor are they "disabled." In Hour 2, I discussed how deaf people perceive themselves as a cultural entity, and have grown to be extremely self-sufficient and independent. You can certainly contribute to the community, but only if you perceive deaf people as your equals at intellectual, physical, and social levels.

Your fluency at the language is also imperative, because deaf people want to be able to communicate easily without having to stop every other word to fingerspell or sign a word for a new signer. Deaf people prefer to be able to communicate fluently, freely, and easily among their peers.

Now, again, this might seem restrictive and might even make you doubt the reality of learning the language. Don't worry. Many deaf people are thrilled to introduce new people into the community, especially because many of them have hearing families, co-workers, and friends.

ATTENTION-GETTING BEHAVIORS

One of the most striking differences between the deaf and hearing communities is how deaf people call each other or try to get each other's attention in a conversation. Because deaf people cannot hear each other, they use various methods of getting each other's attention that often are not seen in the hearing community.

- **Waving one's hand**   The deaf person will wave at the other person. If the other person is across the room, it is perfectly acceptable to wave in a big motion, as long as it's not distracting or interrupting of the situation.

- **Tapping**   This is one of the biggest differences between deaf and hearing communities. In the deaf community, it is perfectly acceptable to touch each other in appropriate places to get attention. For example, one might tap another's shoulders or arms, even if the people do not know each other. In the hearing community, this is frowned upon because of the inappropriateness of touching one another.

- **Flashing lights**   Often at deaf gatherings or in deaf households, lights are flashed on/off to get attention. In the hearing community, this is equivalent to tapping a microphone or saying loudly, "Listen up, people."

- **Third parties**   Oftentimes, a deaf person will be trying to get the attention of another deaf person, but the other person is oblivious to the efforts. The deaf person can then ask someone near that second person to call her or him, and say, "That person over there wants you."

- **Stomping and pounding**   Although this is often restricted to deaf-oriented environments (deaf events, deaf houses, or deaf classrooms), rather than at restaurants or stores, deaf people will pound tables or stomp the floor to get each other's attention. The deaf person feels the vibrations from the pounding or stomping, and he or she will know that someone is trying to get his or her attention.

These are just some of the accepted norms within the deaf community. You might jump or be startled if someone touches your shoulder from behind or stomps the floor next to you. But don't worry, you'll get used to it very fast.

FYI   At deaf weddings—where both the bride and groom are deaf—well-wishers may wave napkins in the air to encourage the newlyweds to kiss. This is akin to tapping glasses at hearing weddings.

BARRIERS

It is a guarantee you will sometimes not understand what a deaf person or other signers are saying, and you might feel flustered or embarrassed. This is normal for anyone learning a new language, and the experience usually becomes a fun memory for you after you become a fluent signer.

When this happens, what should you do? Be honest. Say, "I'm sorry, I don't understand." Often the person will be patient enough to repeat or reword his signs. If it gets to a point where communication seems impossible, resort to different methods: writing back and forth, gesturing, or even getting an interpreter if it's an emergency or serious situation.

You might also have to move to a well-lit area to converse easily. Deaf people often ask for well-lit locations in restaurants or bars, if possible, to make seeing each other for communication more comfortable.

But there's nothing more annoying than finding out that the student didn't understand. Deaf people have often grown up being misunderstood by their families or hearing people, and pretending to understand will only make them feel misunderstood once again. It's better, and more honest, to admit to the signer that you might not be following what he's saying.

LEAVE-TAKING BEHAVIORS

In the English-speaking community, when you need to leave a meeting, class, or conversation for a short bit, the usual procedure is to say, "Excuse me" (when in a conversation) or to leave a meeting or class quietly.

This is also true within a deaf setting, especially in large meetings or classes. However, in smaller gatherings—such as a one-on-one conversation or even class, when you leave, the deaf person will probably look at you quizzically, as if asking, "Where are you going?"

A possible reason for this need to know is hearing people often can hear each other from different rooms in the building, while deaf people cannot. Instead, deaf people choose to inform each other.

So don't be surprised if, as you stand up and leave, you're asked where you're going. It is acceptable to say the reason, or if you don't want to say where, you can simply say you'll be back in a short bit.

MAKING CULTURALLY APPROPRIATE CHOICES

You'll face a lot of situations where you're not sure what is culturally appropriate or best. It is a trial-and-error process, and we learn cultural norms when we make mistakes. Let's look at a few possible scenarios.

POSSIBLE SCENARIO #1

When you come to two signers talking with each other, and you need to pass through, what should you do? Should you find another way around (even if it includes going down the stairs, around the building, and out another door), or should you stand and wait until they finish conversing, hoping they notice you, before passing through?

The answer is neither. You should go ahead and walk through, and if you're the polite type, you can sign "Excuse me" as you walk through. Do not find another way around if it's out of the way. If you choose to stand there watching them and waiting for them to let you through, you will create an uncomfortable feeling for them, almost as if you're gawking at them.

Also, do not crouch down as you walk through (you'd be surprised how many people do this) or draw extra attention to yourself. Signers are used to having people walk between them (although if you *stand* between them, that's a different story).

POSSIBLE SCENARIO #2

What if you're at a store or restaurant, and you see someone signing? Should you approach the deaf person and inform him that you know sign language? Or should you let the deaf person sit in peace and never let on that you know sign?

This is a dilemma that many students and even deaf people themselves face. Some deaf people prefer you approach them, so that they don't sign without knowing anyone can understand them (many embarrassing situations have happened this way!). Yet others prefer to be left alone to their own company. The best answer is to go with what you are comfortable with. If you choose to approach the deaf people, take notice of how the deaf person responds. If the deaf person seems uneager to talk, keep the conversation brief, and excuse yourself.

POSSIBLE SCENARIO #3

You're talking with a deaf person, and are at a comfortable point in the conversation. Suddenly, another hearing person comes up. The hearing person does not know sign, and is trying to communicate with the deaf person. Should you try to interpret?

In most cases, the answer is no. You probably don't yet sign well enough to interpret, and it is the deaf person's decision whether to ask you to help facilitate the conversation or not. If you decide without checking with the deaf person to interpret, you risk sending a message that you think the deaf person isn't able to fend for himself. Let the deaf person guide you to what is the most appropriate action to take. If the hearing person asks you to interpret, check with the deaf person about this.

Whatever scenario you find yourself in, never assume that you know what the deaf person would like to do. Always err on the side of caution, and check with the deaf person if possible before deciding what to do.

GOOD-BYES

Remember how deaf people didn't have access to phones or other helpful technological advances until recently?

This has created a unique cultural tendency: long good-byes. In the old days, because deaf people had such limited time with each other, they'd try to draw out the time together as long as possible. This often resulted in extended goodbyes: A deaf person would first say good-bye to a friend, and see another person he needed to say good-bye to.

By the end of the night, he probably had said good-bye to the entire room, and hours had gone by. The lingering good-byes have continued to this day, even with the new technological options available for deaf people. A majority of deaf people live in the hearing world daily (unless they live in a household with other deaf people), so ASL in a face-to-face setting is a rarity. Even so, it's always enjoyable for deaf people to gather socially and exchange news, gossip, and have fun together.

It is for this reason that many deaf events will end in people standing outside in the parking lots in the process of leaving, still chatting away.

Deaf people often hug each other upon greeting and upon saying good-bye. This is because the deaf community is so close-knit. Deaf people often keep in touch with classmates even from elementary school days, because their paths cross often at national conventions, sporting events, and local events. Hugging is a natural bonding experience, because they are like family.

QUIZ

Hour's Up!

Here's a quiz to help you review some of the facts and ideas presented during this hour. (You can find the correct answers in Appendix A.)

1. The best way to get a deaf person's attention is …

    a. Throw something at him.

    b. Scream loudly at the top of your lungs.

    c. Turn off the lights.

    d. Tap or wave at him.

2. When you meet a deaf person, you should …

    a. Show respect for boundaries, yet be yourself.

    b. Offer to interpret if he needs.

    c. Ask him about specific signs.

    d. Start voicing for him to anyone that approaches.

3. When you see two signers talking and you need to pass through, you should …

    a. Crouch down and walk under their hands.

    b. Find another way around.

    c. Stand and wait until they stop signing.

    d. Walk through.

4. If you see a deaf person at a restaurant, you should …

    a. Go up and introduce yourself.

    b. Say nothing but observe his conversation.

    c. Use your judgment and figure out what the best approach is.

    d. Have the waiter give the deaf person a note saying you know sign language.

5. Two of the cultural tendencies of deaf people, when saying good-bye, are to …

    a. Hug.

    b. Leave immediately.

    c. Shake hands.

    d. Stay for extended periods of times.

6. If you are signing with a deaf person, and a hearing nonsigner approaches your conversation, you should …
   a. Offer to interpret.
   b. Let the deaf person dictate the communication.
   c. Start to interpret.
   d. Leave.

7. True or False: When you need to step outside a meeting or class for a moment, the deaf person might ask you where you're going.

8. If you do not understand what a signer has said, you should …
   a. Nod as if you understand.
   b. Smile.
   c. Inform the signer and ask for clarification.
   d. Walk away.

9. If you, after a few tries, still cannot understand the signer or the signer cannot understand you, what should you do?
   a. Resort to other forms of communication, such as writing back and forth or finding someone to interpret.
   b. Sign the same signs repeatedly until you are understood.
   c. Speak at a louder tone.
   d. Give up.

10. ___ percent of deaf people marry another deaf person.
   a. 15 to 20
   b. 85 to 90
   c. 35 to 40
   d. 65 to 70

QUIZ

RECAP

In this hour, you learned about conversational basics, such as respecting boundaries, getting someone's attention, possible conversational barriers, and leave-taking behaviors. You also learned about typical good-byes and worked through some possible scenarios. Now you're ready to learn how to fingerspell your name.

Hour 5

Learning Your ABCs

LESSON PLAN:

In this hour, you'll learn about ...

- The correct way to fingerspell.
- The finger-spelled alphabet.
- Appropriate uses for finger-spelling.

Some ASL instructors do not support teaching students the finger-spelled alphabet upfront. They feel that learning it before learning the language might create an unnecessary reliance upon the alphabet, especially if one does not know the sign for something. In the event that this happens, the signer usually will only be able to remember the letter when signed in alphabetical order, because he learned it in that method. Rather, they believe the signer should resort to gestures and other methods of communications to express a message if he does not know the actual sign.

With this said, we will go ahead and teach you the alphabet. But please do not use it as your sole method of communicating—it can become very cumbersome to the signer to watch you f-i-n-g-e-r-s-p-e-l-l e-v-e-r-y l-e-t-t-e-r. The rationale in teaching you the alphabet immediately is so you can fingerspell your name when being introduced to a deaf person.

As mentioned earlier, sign language differs from country to country. Fingerspelled versions also vary. Great Britain uses a two-handed version to fingerspell, while Americans use one hand. Even Minnesota has a unique way of fingerspelling *P*, a regional variant, which is rarely seen nowadays.

KNOWING YOUR ABCS

Without much ado, let's learn the alphabet. Be sure to use your dominant hand to fingerspell.

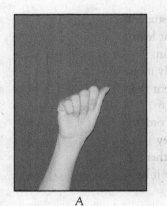
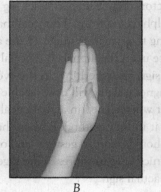
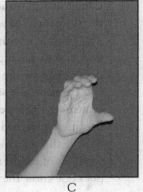

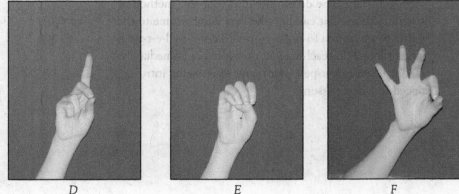

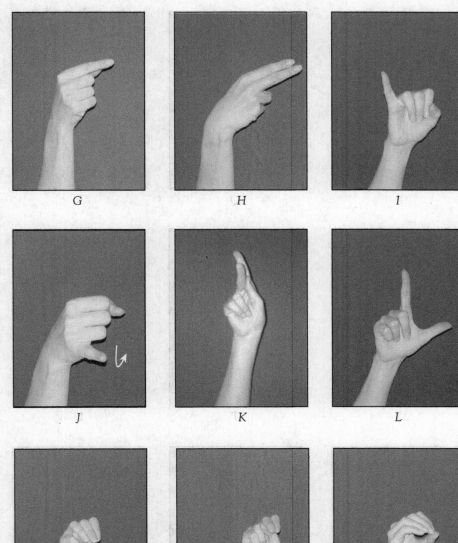

G

H

I

J

K

L

M

N

O

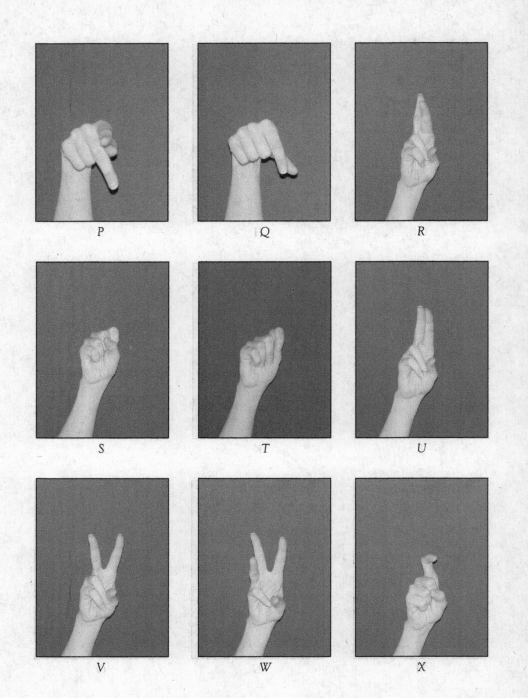

P

Q

R

S

T

U

V

W

X

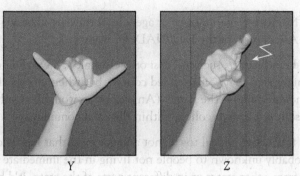

Y   Z

PROCEED WITH CAUTION

Fingerspellers often struggle with the letters *D/F, K/P, A/S, E/O, F/W,* and *M/N.* Be careful not to confuse these letters, because they have similar handshapes but different locations. Other letters that might cause confusion are *A* and *S,* and *O* and *E.*

FINGERSPELLING SMOOTHLY AND CLEARLY

When fingerspelling, your elbow should hang naturally at your side, and your hand should parallel your shoulder. Keep your hand steady, and do not bounce your hand from letter to letter (nor should you nod your head in rhythm with each letter). Just like any other part of ASL, practice is key in learning how to fingerspell smoothly and clearly.

When going from one finger-spelled word to the next word (as you would with your first and last names), you should pause ever so slightly between words, then keep going. Some signers have a slight movement when they go from one word to the next, but the standard is to pause, and slightly nod your head once.

Always have your hand face toward the other person as you fingerspell. Do not look at your hands as you fingerspell; look at the other person instead.

APPROPRIATE USES FOR FINGERSPELLING

There are certain purposes for the use of fingerspelling. There's not always a sign for each English word (just like there's not always an English word for each sign). The following should be fingerspelled:

- Brand names (cars, restaurants, food, and so on).
- Proper names of people and animals.
- Names of locations (towns, schools, stores, and so on).
- Titles of books, publications, and movies.

- Names of organizations or agencies if they are abbreviated (National Association of the Deaf/NAD, for instance).

Some brand names, such as Pepsi or McDonald's, have their own signs. Also, you might sign that you attended college, but when you specify which college, you should spell out the name. (An exception would be Gallaudet University because it is a known college within the Deaf community.)

If you talk about a local town (not a major city) that has its own name sign, it's probably unknown to people not living in the immediate vicinity. To outsiders from other states or in different parts of the state, it'd be better to spell out the town name first, then go ahead and use the name sign. Most major cities have signs, and we'll look at those in Hour 11.

You also should fingerspell your name whenever meeting someone new, even if you have a name sign; although name signs are usually not provided until the second or third meeting.

LEXICALIZED FINGERSPELLING

There are some fingerspelled words in ASL that have become what are called *lexicalized* words. Lexicalized means they become wordlike with its own distinctive movement, or look like an actual sign, but are actually fingerspelled.

In fingerspelling, many words are formed so that they look like a sign, even if they're actually finger-spelled words. To achieve this, one must be fluent at fingerspelling. The list of lexicalized words is long, but some examples include: television (T-V), refrigerator (R-E-F), and car (C-A-R). Notice that lexicalized words usually consist of words with two to five letters when fingerspelling. To best learn lexicalized words, observe native signers and note how they fingerspell specific words.

HANDS-ON PRACTICE

Here are some terrific activities you can do to practice fingerspelling:

- Look in the phone book and fingerspell the names.
- Fingerspell anywhere you see words.
- Fingerspell words you see off billboards, books, and TV.
- Play word games with friends.

A great word game to play is Scrabble. Fingerspell each word you lay down, and if you fingerspell it wrong, you lose points. Make up your own rules.

Aim for clarity rather than speed. With practice you'll gain speed and fluency, but clarity should always be the goal.

HOUR'S UP!

Here's a quiz to help you review some of the facts and ideas presented during this Hour. Some questions have more than one answer. (You can find the correct answers in Appendix A.)

1. True or False: Fingerspelling is key to American Sign Language, and should be used whenever possible.

2. You should fingerspell when …
   a. Giving the name of a town.
   b. Giving dollar amounts.
   c. Giving names of people.
   d. You don't know the sign for something.

3. When fingerspelling, you should signify the end of a word by …
   a. Signing FINISH.
   b. Pausing slightly.
   c. Slashing the air.
   d. You don't signify the end of a word.

4. What does this fingerspell?

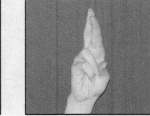

QUIZ

a. Zebra

b. Water

c. Tiger

d. Adapt

5. When fingerspelling, you should strive for …

a. Speed.

b. Beauty.

c. Style.

d. Clarity.

RECAP

In this hour, you took a look at the finger-spelled alphabet, and learned about the different uses for fingerspelling. In the next hour, you'll learn how to sign different variations of numbers and money-related signs.

HOUR 6

Crunching Numbers

LESSON PLAN:

In this hour, you'll learn about ...

- Numbers one through one million.
- Cardinal and ordinal numbers.
- Money signs.

Numbers are another integral part of ASL—and one of the most difficult parts, too. We use numbers to talk about money, time, counting, addresses, phone numbers, heights, places, and many more subjects. In this hour, we'll focus on numbers 1 through 10 first, then discuss the difference between cardinal and ordinal numbers, money signs, and other uses for numbers.

NUMBERS 1 THROUGH 10

Let's hit you with the digits.

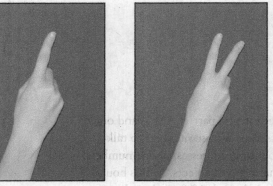

1 2 3

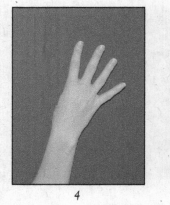

4 5 6

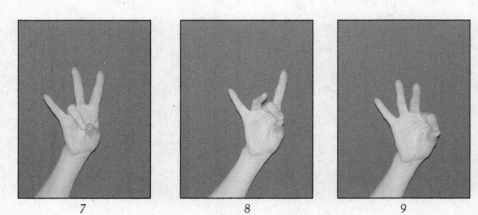

7 8 9

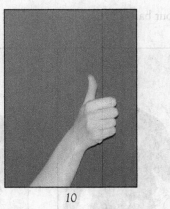

10
Shake your hand slightly.

PROCEED WITH CAUTION

Be sure to practice the signs for numbers six and nine and seven and eight to ensure that they are easily distinguishable. Another number to practice is three; hearing people tend to use the first three fingers instead of the thumb and two fingers that is used in ASL.

CARDINAL AND ORDINAL NUMBERS

As if the numbers weren't hard enough to sign, there's more! Palm orientation is valuable: Sometimes you'll sign numbers facing the other person, and other times it'll be facing yourself. There are specific purposes and specific times for using palm orientation.

There are two types of numbers: cardinal and ordinal. In ASL, these affect the numbers one through five only; numbers six through nine are signed the same way regardless of the type—the palms always face the other person.

When counting things using the numbers between one and five, you will sign with the palm facing yourself. These are called *cardinal* (counting) *numbers*. Two examples of how to use cardinal numbers are shown in the following examples.

I bought four balls.

ME , BUY

FOUR BALL

I have three children.

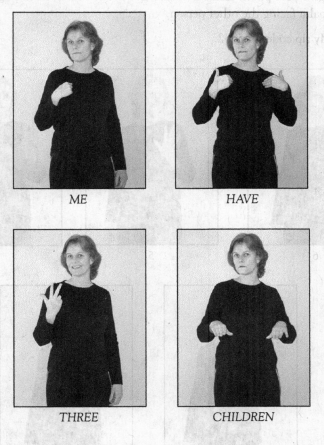

ME

HAVE

THREE

CHILDREN

You use *ordinal numbers* (numbers in a specific order) for situations where you give your phone number or address. Ordinal numbers are signed with the palm facing the other person.

My zip code is 65732.

6   5   7

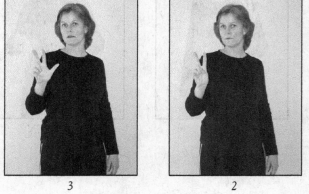

3   2

Ordinal numbers are also used for telling ages. You should sign AGE (which is the same sign as OLD, shown later in this book), then the number (AGE-7, AGE-34). Think you're ready for numbers 11 through 100?

NUMBERS 11 THROUGH 100, 1,000, AND 1 MILLION

For numbers 11 through 29, we've tried to show how each number should be signed in the following pictures. Although there are two pictures for some of the numbers, they should be signed in one motion, rather than separate signs.

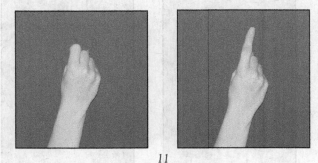

11

Flick the index finger in a repeated motion.

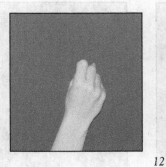 

12

Flick both the index and middle fingers in a repeated motion.

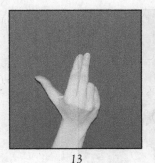 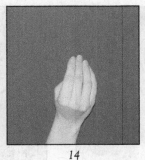 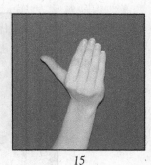

13	14	15
Move your fingers back and forth slightly.	*Move your fingers back and forth slightly.*	*Move your fingers back and forth slightly.*

There are two ways to sign the numbers 16 through 19, so I'll show you the version that most deaf adults or native signers use. The other version not shown here consists of "shaking" the numbers 16 through 19 in a specific fashion.

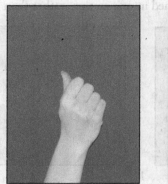 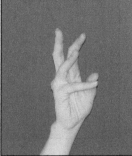

16

 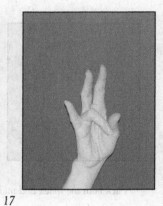

17

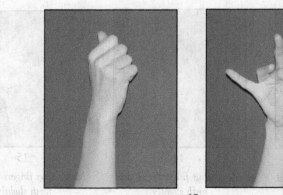 

18

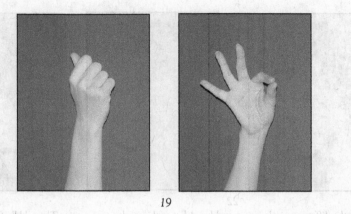

19

As you look at how to sign the numbers 20 through 29, you might wonder why the L handshape is used instead of the 2 handshape. As you know by now, ASL has French influence. The L handshape is how deaf French people sign 2, which is also how we sign the numbers 20 through 29.

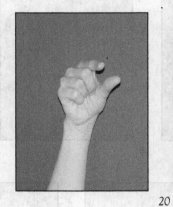 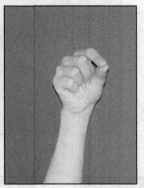

20

21

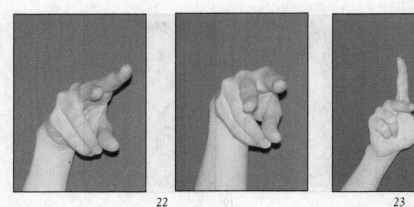

22   23

Note the difference in location and handshape; this is also true for other same-digit numbers (44, 55, and so on).

The middle finger is wiggled slightly.

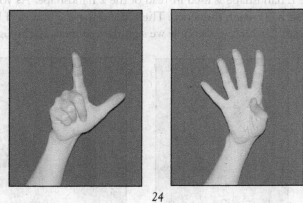

24

 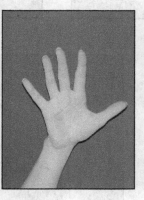 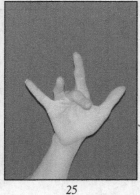

25   25

This is another common way of signing 25; the middle finger is wiggled slightly.

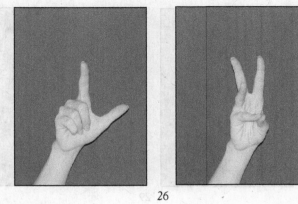

26

27

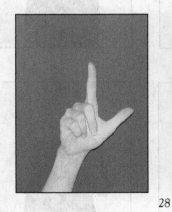

28

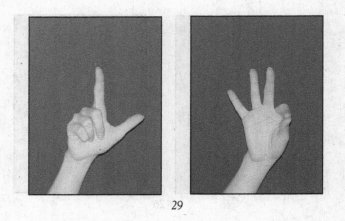

29

The motions are similar for the numbers 30 through 100. The first number is signed, then the second number. I'll show you a few numbers to give you the idea.

30

43

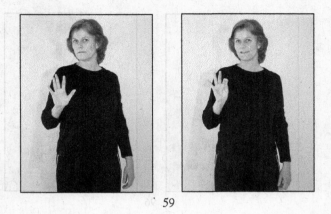

59

For numbers 33, 44, 55, 66, 77, 88, and 99, the way to sign is a slightly different way from the other numbers.

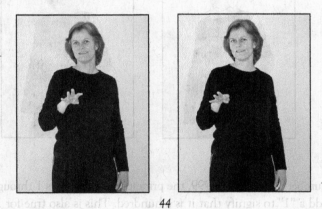

44

Flick your wrist slightly as you go from the first digit to the next.

The numbers 67 through 69, 76 through 79, 86 through 89, and 96 through 98 are signed differently, as well. When the first digit (for example, 96) is higher than the second digit, you twist your wrist slightly downward. If the second digit (for example, 78) is higher than the first digit, you twist your wrist slightly upward.

96

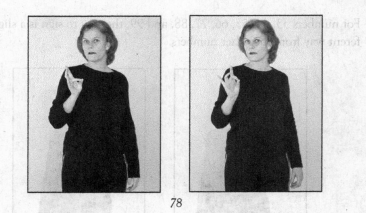

78

For numbers 100 through 999, the principles for numbers 1 through 99 apply, but add a "1" to signify that it is a hundred. This is also true for 200, 300, and so on.

100

To sign 200 or 300, change the 1 handshape to 2 or 3, and so on.

114

Notice the slightly different way of signing 100—this is another way to sign the number, and can be used for numbers 101 through 199.

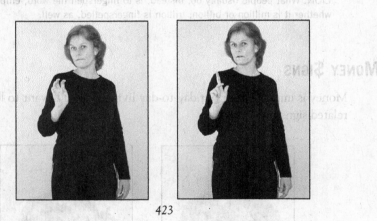

423

For numbers over 1,000 or 1 million, the thousand and million words are also signed differently, but again, the same principles of signing numbers apply. For instance, 2,563 would be signed as TWO THOUSAND FIVE HUNDRED SIXTY-THREE.

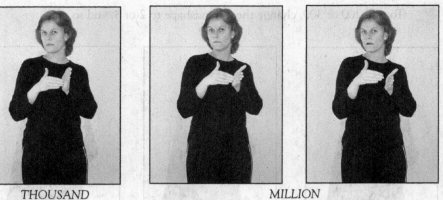

THOUSAND

MILLION

This is very similar to THOUSAND, but with the sign being repeated in a slight upward motion.

FYI With more references to the word billion appearing nowadays—billionaires, populations in the billions—the actual sign is somewhat difficult to distinguish from MILLION. What people usually do, instead, is to fingerspell the word, emphasizing whether it is million or billion; trillion is fingerspelled, as well.

MONEY $IGNS

Money is important for our day-to-day living, so you'll want to learn money-related signs, too.

CENT

The sign for CENT is similar to the sign for THINK, but the motion differs in that the index finger is moved away from the temple.

DOLLAR   COIN

MONEY   CHECK

Bounce the dominant hand
several times.

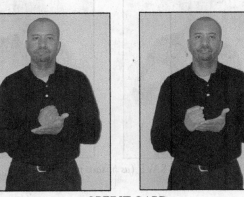

CREDIT CARD

Make a motion as if you are running your card through an older
credit card machine.

DEPOSIT

SIGN (as in sign a check)

SAVE (as in save money)

BORROW

To sign LOAN, you would sign the word in the opposite direction (away from yourself instead of toward yourself).

PAY

BUY

INVEST

HOW MUCH?

HOW MUCH/PRICE/COST

*This sign is commonly used
when asking a question. For
example, "What does that cost?"
or "What's the price on that?"*

COST

The following words are fingerspelled:

ATM   BANK (lexicalized word)   CASH

Dollar amounts may be signed two different ways. The first way is a more formal manner, which would be to sign the number and then DOLLAR. The other way is more common and more casual. Let's use $3.75 as an example.

3 DOLLARS   7   5

Note how the signer swings the number 3 toward himself, rather than signing 3 and DOLLAR separately, and does not sign CENTS. This also is used for other dollar amounts up to $9.99.

With some practice, you'll have the numbers down pat.

QUIZ

HANDS-ON PRACTICE

The phone book is a gold mine of names, numbers, and addresses. Look through them and practice fingerspelling names and numbers at random.

Here are some more practice sentences to fingerspell:

The quick brown fox jumps over the lazy dog.

Pack my box with five dozen liquor jugs.

My phone number is (630) 555-1375.

My zip code is 90148.

That cost $114.36.

I paid $8.76.

Also, look through store aisles and tell your partner how much something costs.

HOUR'S UP!

Here's a quiz to help you review some of the facts and ideas presented during this Hour. Some questions have more than one answer. (You can find the correct answers in Appendix A.)

1. When signing the numbers 20 through 29, you can see the _____ influence on the language?

    a. American

    b. British

    c. French

    d. Swedish

2. How much does a candy bar cost?

a. $1.00

b. $2.00

c. $3.00

d. $10.00

3. You use cardinal numbers when …

a. Counting.

b. Showing orderly numbers.

c. Telling how much of something you have.

d. Giving ages.

4. When saying your phone number, you should …

a. Have your palm face toward yourself.

b. Have your palm face toward the other person.

c. Bounce between numbers to show separation.

d. Swing it over to yourself.

5. What is the following number?

QUIZ

a. 3572
b. 2482
c. 3482
d. 2572

VOCABULARY LIST

Here's a summary of the signs you've learned in this hour:

1 through 100	THOUSAND
MILLION	BILLION
AGE	ATM
BANK	BUY
CASH	CENT
CHECK	COIN
COST	CREDIT CARD
DEPOSIT	DOLLAR
HOW MUCH	INVEST
LOAN	MONEY
PAY	SAVE (MONEY)
SIGN (A CHECK)	

RECAP

In this hour, you learned how to sign different variations of numbers, and learned money-related signs. In the next hour, you'll look at ASL grammar.

Hour 7

A Look at Grammar, Part 1

LESSON PLAN:

In this hour, you'll learn about ...

- Nonmanual signals.
- Topic/comment sentences.
- Yes/no and *Wh*-word questions.
- Rhetorical questions.

For most, grammar is the hardest part of learning a new language. Picking up vocabulary and specific words might be easy, but actually stringing signs together in appropriate order is as difficult as when you first learned English. Even if you sign in English order—also known as contact signing—your signing will look odd and unnatural (much like Spanish words in English order) to the fluent ASL signer. Although it's not possible to include all the grammatical rules found in ASL in this book, I'll provide an overview of some of the more common, fundamental rules.

As you read on, realize two things:

- ASL is *not* broken English, nor is English broken ASL.

- Get rid of all thought of English grammatical rules.

You'll notice that following each picture is the word in capital letters. Even though there is no written form of ASL, there is a way of writing it in English that is nowhere near the actual form of ASL. This is called ASL gloss: Signs are written in their English equivalent (if any), in ASL word order. Let's use "I bought an old, ugly car." In ASL gloss, it would read as:

CAR ME BUY OLD, UGLY.

This might seem like broken English to the nonsigner, but in ASL, when signed it is grammatically correct.

However, it does not include the full range of grammar—it does not include nonmanual signals, motion of signs, or classifiers. There is a form of ASL gloss that linguists or ASL/interpreting students use as a tool to indicate these things, but it still pales in comparison to the actual signed sentences. Because this is a book for beginners, I've elected to leave out the linguistic markers, and placed explanations below each picture, instead. Be sure to notice the nonmanual signals, along with handshapes and locations of the signs.

As you read through this hour, remember that this is only the beginning of a wonderful journey into a new language. It is impossible to cram a language's grammar into one hour, but we hope this chapter will give you a better idea about the basic grammar used in ASL. I'll also include grammar notes throughout the hours when necessary.

NONMANUAL SIGNALS

You learned in Hour 3 that each word in ASL has four parameters: hand-shape, location, movement, and orientation. In addition to these parameters, another important part of each sign is the nonmanual signals, which are markers that indicate what type of sentence or comment is being said.

A necessary requirement in becoming fluent at ASL is using appropriate nonmanual signals—in other words, appropriate facial expressions. This is the thorn in many students' sides when trying to learn the language. For this reason, you'll learn about nonmanual signals before I discuss sentence types commonly found in ASL.

STRICTLY DEFINED

Nonmanual signals are facial expressions that are grammatical units incorporating the eyebrows, mouth, and cheeks, in addition to body-shifting movements and eye gaze that accompany certain signs. These signals play a grammatical role and can change the meaning of a word.

Perhaps the best way to illustrate how important nonmanual signals are in ASL is to show you several different ways to sign using the word UNDER-STAND.

I understand.
The signer nods as her face shows understanding.

I'm not sure I understand.
The signer frowns slightly as she shakes her head and shows that she doesn't quite understand.

I understand, but not completely.
The signer frowns slightly as she nods, but looks unsure.

I don't understand.
The signer frowns fully, shakes her head more emphatically, and shows clearly that she does not understand.

Do you understand?
The signer raises her eyebrows, tilts her head forward slightly, and holds the sign.

One word, five different meanings—all conveyed through facial expressions and movements. These pictures illustrate the importance that you begin working on all aspects of ASL from day one.

Nonmanual signals also include mouth morphemes—mouth movements that accompany ASL signs. This does not mean actual mouthing of the English version of these words, which many signers do, but specific mouth shapes that accompany some words. The list of mouth morphemes is quite long, so I'll include only a few here.

OOO

To show how thin something is, the signer purses his lips, squints his eyes, and cranes his neck forward slightly. This is usually to show how thin, smooth, or small something is. Words that use these nonmanual signals include WIRE, THIN, and FLOOR.

STA

STA is used to demonstrate "over and over again" or "hard." The signer frowns as he signs STRUGGLE in this example, and makes a circular motion as he signs struggle, first clenching his mouth then opening his mouth repeatedly. Words that use this nonmanual signal include WORK, STUDY, and WAIT.

TH

Signing PLAY, the signer sticks out his tongue slightly, to demonstrate playing without paying much attention or care. Other words that use this nonmanual signal include WALK, TATTLETALE, and DRIVE.

Mouth morphemes, like other nonmanual signals, can indicate time, size, length, and other descriptors. The signer's handshapes will match the nonmanual signals. For instance, when doing the OOO mouth morpheme, the signer often will sign it with an F handshape.

PRONOUNS

In ASL, pronouns are usually indicated by the index finger pointing in a specific direction—also known as indexing. Each location of the finger placement represents a different pronoun. Different handshapes (such as the 2 or 3 handshape) may also be used to indicate plurality. You'll be using pronouns in the sentence types, so let's look at how pronouns are signed.

ME/I

YOU

YOU-ALL

This sign is often made with a sweeping motion to indicate all who are present.

HE/SHE/IT/HIM/HER

Point to the person. If the person is not present, the signer can still point to the person as if present, on either side.

WE/US

Point to yourself in a circular motion from one shoulder to another.

THEY

Point to the group in a circular motion.

MY/MINE

Use an open palm instead of an index finger.

YOUR/YOURS

HIS/HER

Note difference between "That's her" (index finger pointing) and "Her brother" (open palm).

THEIR/THEIRS

OUR/OURS

One way to show plural pronouns, in some instances, is to incorporate numbers.

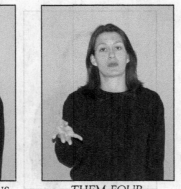

US-TWO/BOTH OF US

THEM-FOUR

If you want to refer to two individuals, you will point to a different location for both persons. For example, if you were saying *she's his sister*, you'd sign it this way:

SHE   HIS   SISTER

Although these aren't pronouns, I'll show you the signs for here and there, because they're often confused with some of the previously shown signs.

THERE   HERE

PROCEED WITH CAUTION

Be aware of what handshape you use when you sign a pronoun. Students often will sign HIS when they mean HE (or THERE for THEIR).

The signer might also point to a place or thing (the English words would be there, that, or it), either within immediate proximity, or at a distance. Notice the nonmanual signals in each picture as well.

That house is mine.

| THAT | HOUSE | MINE |

Pointing or using a Y hand-
shape to say THAT is
acceptable.

To establish gender when signing pronouns, the signer will usually point to the person (whether the person is there or not), and sign GIRL or BOY (or WOMAN or MAN). Another way to establish gender is to indicate it by a separate lexical item, such as a name or a gender-specific word.

That woman is my mother.

| SHE | MY | MOTHER |

John is starving!

HE HUNGRY

The signer is pointing to John as he signs HUNGRY. However, if John was not present in the room and John has not been mentioned prior to the statement, the signer would fingerspell John's name to establish whom he's talking about. Note the nonmanual signals, such as the frown, on the signer's face; they show how hungry John is.

Topic/Comment Structure

In ASL, ideas and thoughts are expressed using specific structures. One of the more common sentence types is the topic/comment structure, where the topic is first identified, then followed by the comment. Topic/comment structures are often used as a form of organizing words, especially in longer sentences or questions.

The following pictures show an example of a topic/comment sentence. The signer will raise his eyebrows and tilt his head forward slightly as he says the topic, then move the head back and allow his eyebrows to lower when saying the comment.

I like ice cream.

ICE CREAM	ME	LIKE
The signer keeps her eyebrows raised as she signs ICE CREAM (which is the topic).		*The signer returns her eyebrows to their normal places, moves her head back slightly and nods as she says ME LIKE—establishing the comment.*

Using the topic/comment structure is a good way to establish topics and give the listener the necessary hints about the type of sentence being said.

YES/NO QUESTIONS

When you are asked a question that requires either a yes or no answer, the signer will do a few specific things to show you he or she is expecting a yes/no answer.

The signer will have his eyebrows raised, making eye contact with you, with his head tilted slightly forward, and hold the last sign while awaiting a response.

Is he deaf?

HE   DEAF?

The signer keeps her eyebrows raised throughout the sentence, showing that she is asking a question. The last word is also held awaiting a response.

Are you deaf?

YOU   DEAF?

If you see the signer using these nonmanual signals, then chances are it's a question that requires a yes or no answer. You might also see a question mark signed at the end, although the sign isn't necessary. The question mark is already incorporated in the actual sentence by the raised eyebrows and other nonmanual signals.

There are two ways to use the question mark sign. The first is to show doubt or disbelief. This can be used as an actual question, or as a conversational indicator.

SURE? (Are you sure?)

The signer squints her eyes, tilts her head down once, and wiggles her crooked finger as she holds her head in place.

The second way is to show shock or surprise.

REALLY! (Wow, really?!)

WH- WORD QUESTIONS

For *Wh-* word questions—questions that ask why, where, when, who, what, or how—the method is slightly different. The signer will frown slightly, narrow his or her eyes slightly, and tilt his or her head forward a little. He will again make eye contact with you, and hold the last sign waiting for your answer.

Why didn't you show up?

NOT

SHOW-UP

WHY?

The following figures show the signs for WHO, WHAT, WHEN, WHERE, WHY, and HOW.

WHY

WHY

Using 4 fingers instead of
only one.

WHERE

WHO

WHEN

WHAT   HOW

You might see some fluent signers fingerspelling the words WHAT and WHEN as an exclamation, although one needs to be fluent at ASL before attempting to do this.

Another common question that has become a sign is "What do we do?" or "What are you doing?" The nonmanual signals are the same as for *Wh-* word questions.

DO-DO?

RHETORICAL QUESTIONS

Another common type of sentence in ASL is the rhetorical question, which is similar to the topic/comment sentence. The signer will sign a question, then answer it in the same sentence. The word *because* isn't used often in

ASL, because the word is replaced by the question and the answer that comes afterward. There are two types of rhetorical questions: yes/no rhetorical questions, and *Wh-* word rhetorical questions. However, rhetorical questions have different nonmanual signals from *Wh-* word questions: The eyebrows are raised, instead of furrowed.

In rhetorical questions, the signer holds the last word in the question, eyebrows raised. Then as he or she proceeds to answer his or her own question, the signer nods slightly, and the eyebrows return to their normal position.

I went to the store because I left my keys there.

ME

GO

STORE

WHY?

The eyebrows are raised when saying this word, and the signer tilts her head forward slightly.

KEYS

The eyebrows return to normal position.

LEFT

Notice how the signer shows appropriate emotion (disappointment or frustration) when she says she left her keys at the store. In the following example, take another look at the nonmanual signals.

We're eating at my home.

EAT

WHERE?

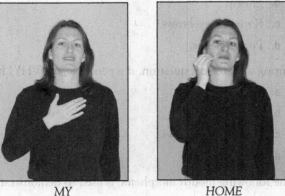
MY   HOME

HOUR'S UP!

Here's a quiz to help you review some of the facts and ideas presented during this hour. Some of the questions have more than one answer. (You can find the correct answers in Appendix A.)

1. True or False: ASL has its own grammatical rules that are separate and different from English's grammatical rules.

QUIZ

2. Mouth morphemes are …

    a. Part of English.

    b. Mouth movements that accompany ASL signs.

    c. Mouth movements that accompany English words.

    d. Not part of ASL.

3. A topic/comment sentence is demonstrated by …

    a. Frowning while saying the topic, then raising the eyebrows during the comment.

    b. Squinting your eyes throughout the entire statement.

    c. Keeping your eyebrows raised throughout the statement.

    d. Raising your eyebrows while saying the topic, then lowering the eyebrows during the comment.

4. During a *Wh-* word question, the signer will …

    a. Smile.

    b. Frown.

    c. Raise his eyebrows.

    d. Purse his lips.

5. During a rhetorical question, if a person signs WHY? he will …

    a. Smile.

    b. Frown.

    c. Raise his eyebrows.

    d. Purse his lips.

6. The following mouth morpheme is used to demonstrate …

    a. Something being done over and over.

    b. Something being big in size.

    c. Something being small in size.

    d. Carelessness.

7. True or False: Nonmanual signals and movements can alter the meaning of a word completely.

8. To show possession (his, her, mine, yours), the signer should ...

    a. Use the index finger.

    b. Use a closed fist.

    c. Use two open palms.

    d. Use an open palm.

9. Signers may demonstrate plurality in pronouns by ...

    a. Incorporating numbers into the sign.

    b. Counting before signing.

    c. Setting up spatial relationships.

    d. Doing nothing. You can't show plurality in pronouns.

10. When does the signer hold his last sign?

    a. Topic/comment

    b. Rhetorical questions

    c. Yes/no questions

    d. *Wh-* word questions

QUIZ

RECAP

There are many ways to formulate a sentence or question in ASL. You examined nonmanual signals, topic/comment sentences, and different types of questions. In the next hour, you'll look at more ASL grammatical rules.

HOUR 8

A Look at Grammar, Part 2

LESSON PLAN:

In this hour, you'll learn about ...

- Negations and assertions.
- Directional verbs.
- Conditional sentences.
- Adjectives.
- Commands.

You've learned how different questions require the use of specific nonmanual signals. You've also seen how various markers, such as nonmanual signals and movements, can alter the meaning of the words. Understanding these grammatical aspects is a crucial step to developing fluency at ASL.

MAKING NEGATIONS AND ASSERTIONS

Just as a person can speak in different tones to show the degree of negation (No, Noooo, NO!) or to show assertion, a signer can sign in different ways to show how much of a negation or assertion the word is.

When you answer a yes or no question, there are specific ways to respond. Normally, in an introduction situation, you will not need to involve a lot of facial expression in your yes/no responses, but here are some examples of how to answer a question with different degrees of assertion or negation.

Yes, he's here.

YES   HERE

The signer nods while signing HERE.

Yes, he's here!

YES   HERE!

*Note the frown on the
signer's face.*

Nodding rapidly and frowning slightly shows an emphasis on the response.

Yes, he's here!

YES   HERE

The signer's exaggerated nonmanual signals show that there's no way the person isn't here.

No, he's not here.

NO   NOT   HERE

The signer shakes his head slightly while signing politely that the person is not here.

No, he's not here!

NO   NOT   HERE

The signer looks firm in his response, shaking his head more emphatically while signing. He also tilts his head while shaking his head no, with narrowed eyes and furrowed brows.

Maybe he's here, I'm not sure.

MAYBE   NOT   SURE

The signer shows that he is not sure by slightly shrugging and shaking his head slowly, showing a look of uncertainty at the same time.

Negations are how you make a sentence negative. There are different ways to negate or assert a comment (as you saw in the previous examples): signing the appropriate negative word (not, no, none, and so on), and/or shaking your head no. The signer often will either squint or frown as he shakes the head no and usually has a raised upper lip.

I haven't seen anyone.

SEE   NONE

The same rules apply to assertions—when a person confirms or asserts that something is true. Usually, a signer will nod repeatedly to assert that something did happen or will happen.

If the person is trying to assert something with force, he or she might frown as he signs yes, or fingerspell Y-E-S emphatically. People also often sign TRUE as they nod rapidly to say, "Yes, it's a fact!" when challenged by someone else's doubts.

USING DIRECTIONAL VERBS (SUBJECT-OBJECT AGREEMENT)

Another way to use verbs in ASL is using them as directional verbs (also called subject-object agreement by many ASL linguists). In directional verbs, the meaning of the verb depends on the verb's movement and location. Spatial locations play a major role in this type of verb usage. I'll use the word *give* for our examples. First, the sign for GIVE:

GIVE

In each of the following sentences, the one-handed version of GIVE is used. Take note of the directionality in each picture, and notice how people's positions have been established.

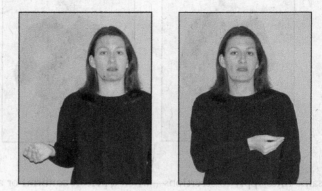

She gave him a book.

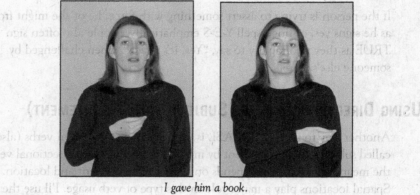

I gave him a book.

I gave her a book.

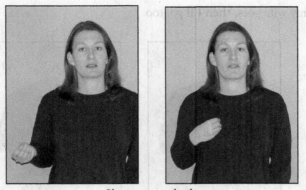

She gave me a book.

In each of these examples, the same sign is used, but it moves in different directions. This is how spatial relationships are set up (who is standing where), and this is how we know who gave the book to whom.

SIGNING CONDITIONAL SENTENCES

Conditional sentences are when the topic being discussed has a condition or conditions. In English, conditions are expressed by the word "if" or "suppose." Although the words can certainly be signed, they aren't necessary, because they can be expressed through nonmanual signals. The condition is usually signed with raised eyebrows, and the consequence has lowered eyebrows.

If nobody shows up, I'm leaving.

NONE | ME | LEAVE

The signer raises his eyebrows, tilting his head forward slightly.

The signer has his eyebrows in normal position, and moves his head back slightly.

If my wife goes, then I'll go, too.

WIFE

*Eyebrows are raised, head
tilted forward.*

GO

*Eyebrows are still raised and
the head is still tilted.*

ME

GO

*The head moves back, and
the eyebrows return to normal position. The signer also
nods as he signs ME GO.*

GIVING COMMANDS

We all give commands at one time or another. In ASL, the way a signer
gives commands is somewhat similar to how commands are spoken in
English. Often, in giving a command, a person will leave out the subject.
This is true in ASL, too.

Signing commands are usually formed using sharper, clearer handshapes with sharpness in motion.

The intensity of the command is also expressed through nonmanual signals, which include direct eye contact. The following photo shows the word *sit* as a direct command.

SIT!
The signer frowns and the
hands are tense.

In the previous command, you can see that the signer means business. The seriousness of the command is detected through nonmanual signals. The command form can be used for longer sentences (*I told you to go sit down right now!*) and for a wide variety of words.

BUILDING SENTENCES WITH VERBS

In ASL, sentences with verbs tend to follow a structure of Subject + Verb + Object. Also, verbs in ASL do not have past or future tenses attached to them like they do in the English language. Separate signs, such as FINISH, YESTERDAY, or WILL, demonstrate the tenses. We'll explore temporal aspects more in Hour 19 when we discuss time, but here's an example:

The man went fishing.

MAN

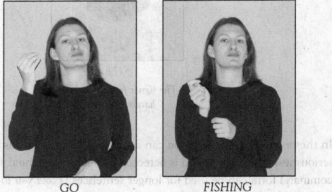

GO   FISHING

Sentences with verbs can follow a structure of Object + Subject + Verb.

It should be noted that movement distinguishes verbs from nouns that have the same meaning or handshape. For example, the word *paint* can be used as either a noun or a verb; signing it once shows that it is a noun, but repeated motions show that it is a verb. The same is true for words such as open/door (same handshape, different motion), sit/chair, mow/lawnmower, and so on. Nouns often have repeated quick movements, and verbs usually have one deliberate movement.

USING ADJECTIVES

In sentences that include adjectives, the adjectives may appear before or after the nouns or verbs, although it seems to be more common to place the adjective after the noun. Adjectives are shown by using nonmanual signals and signs, and usually are signed as the comment when using the topic/comment structure.

That car is very old.

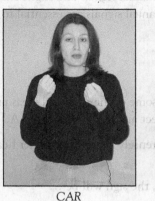

CAR

The signer raises her eyebrows to establish topic (car).

OLD

The intensity of the signer's nonmanual signals shows how old the car is. She squints her eyes and frowns slightly.

Adjectives can also be different, according to the emphasis and rhythm of the sign motion, and nonmanual signals. For example, the following signer shows the difference in a boy's height.

TALL

The signer's mouth morpheme, facial expression, and placement of the handshape show how tall the person is—in this case, not much taller than her.

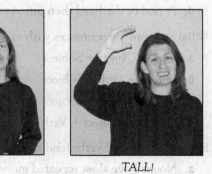

TALL!

The nonmanual signals here are dramatically different, and the handshape is placed at a higher location.

The meaning and concept of the same word becomes wholly different through a simple change in nonmanual signals and slight change in location of the sign. For adjectives, nonmanual signals are essential to indicate the intensity or degree.

HOUR'S UP!

QUIZ

Here's a quiz to help you review some of the facts and ideas presented during this hour. (You can find the correct answers in Appendix A.)

1. True or False: The more intensely a person nods her head, the more intense her assertion is.

2. When a command is made, the sign will be …
   a. In repeated motions.
   b. In a soft, gentle motion.
   c. In a tense, abrupt motion.
   d. In exaggerated motions.

3. Conditional sentences are signed with …
   a. Furrowed eyebrows then a nod of the head.
   b. Raised eyebrows then lowered eyebrows.
   c. Lowered eyebrows then raised eyebrows.
   d. A nod of the head then furrowed eyebrows.

4. What structure do sentences with verbs tend to follow in ASL?
   a. Verb + Object + Subject
   b. Object + Verb + Subject
   c. Subject + Verb + Object
   d. Subject + Object + Verb

5. How do nouns and verbs tend to differ in signing?
   a. Nouns have slow, repeated movements, and verbs have quick, repeated movements.
   b. Nouns are made with a quick motion, and verbs are made with a slow motion.
   c. Nouns are made with quick, repeated motions, and verbs are made with a deliberate motion.
   d. Nouns are made with one motion, and verbs have quick, repeated motions.

6. What answer is the signer giving?

- **a.** Yes, I'm definite.
- **b.** No, that's not true!
- **c.** Are you serious?!
- **d.** Maybe, I'm not sure.

7. What type of sentence is the signer saying?

a. Rhetorical question

b. Conditional statement

c. Topic/comment

d. Command

8. True or False: Signing a question mark can show disbelief or shock.

9. When does an adjective usually appear in a sentence?

a. Before the noun or verb

b. After the noun or verb

c. After the verb

d. Either before or after the noun or verb

10. True or False: In directional verbs, spatial locations play a minor role.

RECAP

In this hour, you examined negations/assertions, directional verbs, conditional sentences, adjectives, and commands. In the following hour, you'll learn how to introduce yourself when meeting deaf people.

PART III

Holding a Conversation

HOUR 9

Introducing Yourself

LESSON PLAN:

In this hour, you'll learn about ...

- What to do when you meet a deaf person.
- Typical introductions.
- Name signs.

Now that you've learned fingerspelling, numbers, and basic grammatical rules, you'll want to start meeting deaf people. It's understandable if you feel awkward or uncomfortable about actually interacting with deaf people, especially when your ASL skills probably are nonexistent or minimal. You also might be worried that you'll make some mistakes or say culturally inappropriate things.

When you meet a deaf person—and this applies to any new person you meet for the first time—relax and be yourself. That sounds cliché, but it works. Although it might be your first time meeting a deaf person, it's not the deaf person's first time meeting a hearing person. In many cases, he will guide you through the introduction and make you feel at ease. Get ready to explore the various aspects of introductions within the Deaf community.

MEETING A DEAF PERSON

As you've read by now, the Deaf community is so close-knit, so newcomers are often looked upon with curiosity. Don't be surprised if the deaf person starts asking you a bunch of questions about your background. Deaf people do this when meeting each other for the first time, too.

The questions they ask each other upon meeting are generally background related, such as, "Where are you from?" or asking what schools they attended, whether they know so-and-so. This is so they can establish a common bond in their experiences, and because many deaf people know other deaf people all over the country. Here's a typical conversation between two deaf people meeting for the first time.

Jim: Hi, I'm Jim Smith.

Mary: Nice to meet you. My name's Mary Bailey. Where are you from?

Jim: I'm from Washington, D.C. You?

Mary: I'm from Florida, but I went to Gallaudet in D.C.

Jim: So did I! What year did you graduate? I'm from the class of 1975.

Mary: I graduated in 1995, but my parents were also class of 1975ers. Do you know Alan and Jean Bailey? Dad was from North Carolina, and Mom was from Illinois.

Jim: Oh, wasn't your dad the brother of Steve? Yes, I know him! He lived across the hall from me in the dorm!

With this introductory conversation, Jim and Mary know they have shared acquaintances and experiences so they are able to quickly form a new friendship. Because you are new to the community and an ASL student, you probably will be asked about what brought you to learn the language and what you hope to do with the language. Deaf people are sometimes wary of hearing people who learn the language "because it's a beautiful language" or "because I want to help deaf people." They might feel that they do not need help, and wonder about people's motivations in learning the language.

The wariness is probably because years and years of misguided desires to help "the deaf" have accomplished very little in terms of providing equal access for deaf people. Some signers have even declared themselves "interpreters" after only one or two ASL classes—which isn't only unfair to deaf people, it's also dangerous in situations where the signer cannot understand what is being said or cannot sign fluently what is being voiced. This can become a life or death situation, which is discussed further in Hour 14.

The most important element you can bring with you to the conversation is sincerity.

TYPICAL INTRODUCTIONS

Suppose you're at a deaf event, and your ASL teacher introduces you to another deaf person. What should you expect her to say to the deaf person?

The teacher probably will say to the deaf person, "This is Nancy, and she's hearing. She's taking ASL with me, and lives in Milwaukee, but she grew up in Chicago and has a deaf brother." You might feel the introduction is a bit drawn-out, but it serves a purpose.

The information tells the deaf person that you're learning sign and not yet fluent; that you're hearing; what your involvement with the deaf community is; and where you are from. The deaf person can now ask you about your class, who your brother is, or if you know so-and-so in Milwaukee; and best of all, he will probably sign slower to meet your fluency level. Carol Padden, a well-known deaf researcher, author, and educator, writes that this information-giving ritual is a way of preserving group cohesiveness.

Here are some tips for when you meet a deaf person:

- Never apologize for your signing or mistakes. It's okay if you flub your signs. You are a student of the language, after all.
- Don't fake understanding a person's signs. If you do not understand, say so; there's nothing deaf signers dislike more than students of the language faking comprehension.
- Maintain eye contact, especially if you hear something happening elsewhere or someone calls your name. If you have to look away, be sure to indicate "hold on" by holding up your index finger, or explain what is happening. Remember, the deaf person does not know what you are hearing as you two chat, and it's impolite for you to suddenly look away without explanation. It also might give the deaf person a sense of being left out if something takes place unbeknownst to him.
- Maintain eye contact with the signer rather than watching the hands moving as the signer is talking. This makes you look as if you're watching a bee flying around.

JUST A MINUTE

When you are conversing with a signer, the appropriate place to gaze is in the general area from the head to the chest. Do not watch only the signs—you will miss important language and facial signals.

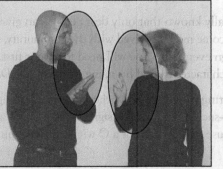

The typical area to gaze at during a conversation is shaded in gray.

Oddly enough, some ASL students ask deaf people how to pronounce a name if the name is unique. Obviously, this isn't appropriate, especially if the deaf person does not speak. A deaf woman with a unique name says, "Whenever people ask me how to pronounce my name, I look at them and say, 'Why should I care? I sign, not speak!' That usually makes them realize the silliness of their request, and I always tell them it's alright."

Name Signs

When you are introduced to someone, you might feel some apprehension at fingerspelling your name and want to invent a name sign for yourself. Many signers also mistakenly believe that every word must have a sign, and that it's not acceptable to fingerspell (or they feel it's too difficult to fingerspell). This goes against cultural boundaries, and should not take place. Remember what happened to Holly Daniel, the woman who invented the sign for a Saturn car? I don't want that to happen to you! Inventing signs—or name signs—is not something a hearing person should do.

Name signs are very much a part of the Deaf community, even in other countries. American deaf people are somewhat unique in their name signs, though: In addition to using descriptive name signs, the use of initialized name signs (also known as arbitrary signs) is also acceptable for a name sign. In other countries, they usually do not use initialized signs for name signs, choosing to use descriptive signs instead. For instance, Laurent Clerc's name sign was an H handshape going back across the cheek, because he had a scar on his cheek.

Not everyone has a name sign, but those who have grown up in the Deaf community usually have one. Typical locations for name signs are at the forehead, on the chest, on the arm, or on the chin. A name sign may not be located in unusual locations, such as the back of the neck or on your ankle.

It is generally known that only deaf people can give new signers a name sign. As you become more involved with the community, you probably will be given a name sign eventually. You will need to earn it first, though, much like Kevin Costner's character earned his name in the movie *Dancing with Wolves*.

Many hearing people inappropriately form name signs that are motion-oriented—such as an L in the sign for "music," or an M going down your head because of long hair, or a C wiggling over the nose because you're "silly." Nor should a name sign be derived from the sound of the name. These simply are not culturally or linguistically appropriate.

Name signs also usually are contained within a specific group. For instance, a name sign might be known only within a school, or a family. In rare instances name signs are known nationally—especially those of well-known deaf leaders or actors. For people not belonging to that immediate group, it's better to fingerspell the name before using the name sign.

When you meet someone new, do not assume that person has a name sign, nor assume that the deaf person knows all your friends' name signs. You should fingerspell your name, and if you are eventually given a name sign, include it after fingerspelling. However, the name sign is often not shown until the second or third meeting.

FYI A terrific resource on name signs is Dr. Sam Supalla's book, *Name Signs*. The book gives us an in-depth look at name signs, including those found within deaf families.

Another difference between the Deaf community and the hearing community is that deaf people often do not refer to each other directly by name, like hearing people do. Hearing people often will talk like this:

Peter, I think you might want …

It's so good to see you, Joan.

Nice to meet you, Jenny.

These are statements of politeness and a way of indicating to whom you're speaking. In ASL, this way of referring to someone by name is pointless because you're usually looking at the person as you sign, so that person already knows you're speaking to him. So, when you meet someone, it's probably better if you don't say, "Nice to meet you, *Jenny*." It'll look awkward, and feel odd for the deaf person. Just "Nice to meet you" will do.

We explored basic grammatical rules in Hour 7, so you should be able to carry on a conversation after some practice. But first, you probably need to learn some signs.

YES

This sign is made with repetitive motions.

NO

This sign is usually made with repetitive motions, although doing it once shows emphasis (such as in commands).

MAYBE

This sign is usually accompanied by a look of uncertainty; repeat motion.

NICE   MEET

The index fingers show two people meeting.

YOU

DON'T KNOW

Move the hand away from your head in a smooth motion.

DON'T UNDERSTAND

Shake your head and frown slightly.

AGAIN/REPEAT

(Could you repeat that? Say that again?)

Frown slightly and show that you didn't understand.

NOT

The thumb begins at the chin and is brought out.

SURE

MY

NAME

SORRY

Move the sign in a circular motion on the chest.

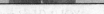

FORGET

OH-I-SEE

Bounce the Y handshape slowly in the air.

HOW

YOU? (How are you?)

GOOD

MORNING

GOOD

NIGHT

FINE

*Bounce the 5 handshape on
your chest two or three times.*

ENJOY

YOURSELF?

(Are you enjoying yourself?)

HEARING

*The motion shows a person
speaking.*

DEAF

*Some people bring the index finger from ear to mouth; others
bring it from mouth to ear. Either way is fine.*

HANDS-ON PRACTICE

Here are some terrific activities you can do to practice what you have
learned:

- Find a fluent signer to practice introducing yourself with, and if possible,
  have him or her take you to meet other deaf people.

- Practice the following dialogue with a partner. Be sure to sign it in
  ASL, not in English order. Remember to incorporate nonmanual signals, especially when you ask questions.

1. Introduce yourself. (MY NAME _____)
2. Ask if your partner is deaf or hearing.
3. Tell your partner you are hearing.
4. If your partner says something you do not understand, express your confusion.
5. Tell your partner it has been nice to meet him or her.

HOUR'S UP!

Here's a quiz to help you review some of the facts and ideas presented during this hour. Some of the questions have more than one answer. (You can find the correct answers in Appendix A.)

1. When you meet a deaf person for the first time, you should …

   a. Be extra-nice and helpful.

   b. Be quiet and let him take the lead.

   c. Be yourself and relax.

   d. Be frightened and leave.

2. True or False: A typical introduction between two signers might include information on the person's background, including family, friends, education, and location.

3. If you do not understand what the signer has just said, you should …

   a. Nod.

   b. Look away.

   c. Say nothing.

   d. Let the signer know you didn't understand.

4. When you are conversing, the appropriate place to direct your gaze is …

   a. In the general area from the head to the chest.

   b. On the signs.

   c. At the person's face.

   d. On the chest.

5. True or False: You can invent your own name sign or ask to be given one.

6. Who can give you a name sign?

   a. Hearing signers

   b. Hearing teachers

   c. Deaf signers

   d. Anyone that comes up with one

7. Name signs in America are ...

   a. Arbitrary.

   b. Nonarbitrary.

   c. Arbitrary and descriptive.

   d. Nonarbitrary and descriptive.

8. True or False: When you are introduced to an ASL user, the name should be introduced in the sentence (*Nice to meet you, John*).

9. If you aren't sure how to pronounce a deaf signer's name, you should ...

   a. Ask the deaf person how to pronounce it.

   b. Repeat it until you're sure you've pronounced it right.

   c. Ask another person, preferably hearing, how to pronounce it.

   d. Not worry about pronunciation; rather, focus on fingerspelling it clearly.

10. When someone asks you why you are learning ASL, you should *not* say ...

   a. Because I want to help deaf people.

   b. I want to use it so I can talk behind people's backs and not have them hear me.

   c. I want to learn the language and culture because it fascinates me.

   d. I feel sorry for people who can't speak, so I want to speak for them.

VOCABULARY LIST

Here's a summary of the signs you've learned in this hour:

YES	NO
MAYBE	AGAIN/REPEAT
DEAF	DON'T KNOW

DON'T UNDERSTAND	ENJOY YOURSELF?
FINE	FORGET
GOOD MORNING	GOOD NIGHT
HEARING	HOW YOU
MY NAME	NICE MEET YOU
NOT SURE	OH-I-SEE
SORRY	

RECAP

In this hour, you've explored the basics of introductions between you and a deaf person using ASL. In the next hour, you'll explore how to exchange personal information in a typical conversation using ASL.

HOUR 10

Sharing Personal Information

CHAPTER SUMMARY

LESSON PLAN:

In this hour, you'll learn about ...

- Being asked if you are deaf or hearing.
- Typical information shared.
- Conversational indicators.

You've learned how to fingerspell your name and what to expect when meeting a deaf person for the first time. After you've been introduced or have met a deaf person, a conversation will naturally progress.

Don't be surprised if the signer immediately asks you if you are deaf or hearing. There's a reason for this: to identify your experiences within the Deaf community. If you are hearing, then the deaf person knows that you do not have all the experiences that a deaf person has had. The deaf person might also be curious as to why you're learning ASL, and begin asking you about this.

Most of the time, you can certainly ask the deaf person about how or when he became deaf, because this will give you an idea of his cultural and linguistic upbringing. But it's not a good idea to ask about how much of a hearing loss he has, or what his current hearing level is. Even though most deaf people have some hearing (it is rare that a person is completely, 100 percent deaf), hearing levels are not of interest nor concern in the Deaf community. This is a "hearing" view, and virtually useless to a deaf person's needs.

In the Deaf community, as long as a deaf person interacts with other deaf people in cultural and social circles, he is considered Deaf.

PROCEED WITH CAUTION

If you are hearing, be sure not to hide this fact from the deaf person. Usually, your signing will give you away, but there are many cases where a fluent signer does not identify that he is hearing until the deaf person finds out at a later point. Many deaf people feel betrayed or fooled (even if this is not your intention) if they don't find out immediately that you're hearing. It's always a good idea to mention it in an introduction somehow.

BACKGROUND EXCHANGE

As mentioned previously, the deaf person will be curious about your involvement with the Deaf community. Do not feel embarrassed if you have no reason other than being interested in the language and culture—these are perfectly acceptable reasons.

When you ask the deaf person about his background, more often than not, the deaf person will be happy to share his educational experiences and background. In most cases, the deaf person's upbringing has shaped his current feelings and values within the Deaf community. Hours 11, 20, and 23 present examples of other information commonly exchanged during this initial conversation (such as family and occupation), but some useful signs you might need in this type of conversation are listed with their signs in the following figures.

FYI

In English, there are different registers of speaking. You might speak formally in a work situation, but speak informally in a social or home environment. The same is true for ASL. Some signs are more formally used in specific situations. Take STUDENT for example. The formal version is:

STUDENT

However, over time, it has evolved so that the following signs are accepted:

 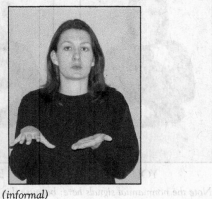

STUDENT *(informal)*

The first version is still used, but mainly in formal situations.

WANT

Start with a 5 handshape, then bend the fingers and bring the hands toward yourself.

LEARN

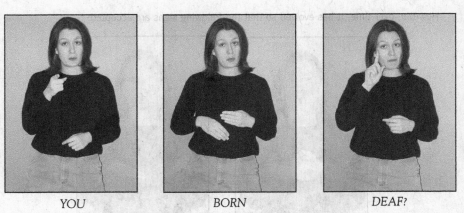

YOU   BORN   DEAF?

Note the nonmanual signals here; because this is a question requiring a yes or no answer, the signer has raised eyebrows and holds the last sign.

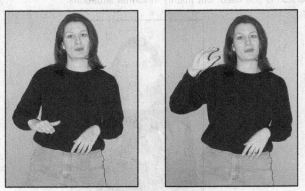

GROW-UP *(raised, grew up)*

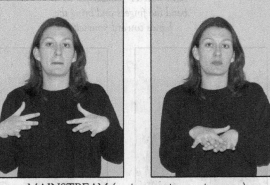

MAINSTREAM *(mainstreaming, mainstream)*

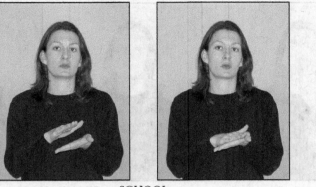

SCHOOL

The fingers may be either spread apart or closed together.

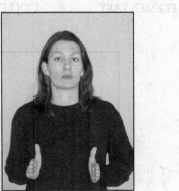

DEAF SCHOOL (*residential school*)

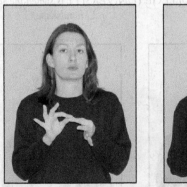

INTERPRETER

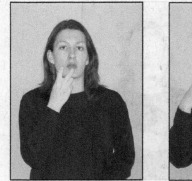

ORAL

HIGH SCHOOL

Make a circular motion around the mouth with a BENT-V handshape.

ELEMENTARY

COLLEGE (UNIVERSITY *is signed the same way, with a U handshape*)

GRADUATION

CONVERSATIONAL INDICATORS

When you hold a conversation with someone—deaf or hearing—you usually provide conversational responses that indicate you're listening and comprehending the dialogue. Hearing people often murmur "Mm-mm" or "Oh?"

In ASL, there are also conversational indicators, although they might seem awkward to the novice signer at first. The most common and necessary indicator is to nod your head at appropriate intervals as you listen.

When you take an ASL class or talk to a deaf person, the deaf person might ask if you understand if there are not visible conversational indicators, such as nodding. Nodding is a way to show the signer you understand what is being said and are following without a problem.

If you do not give appropriate responses, the deaf person will immediately assume you are not following, and ask why you didn't say so or if you understand. Remember the assertions and negations you learned in Hour 7? This is a good time to use them, as well.

If you are not clear about what the signer is saying, be sure to stop and let him know. When you want to interrupt, simply raise your hand out at mid-chest toward the signer, and furrow your eyebrows to show that you're confused.

This is an example of how to interrupt a conversation if you do not understand what is being said.

Some conversational indicators were shown in Hour 8, but others are shown in the following figures. Take note of the nonmanual signals again.

REALLY?

WOW

Move the handshape left and right in a straight line. (If this sign is made with a sad or dismayed look, it probably means, "Oh, that's terrible!")

GOOD

Some people use two hands for the sign for GOOD, although the sign has evolved to the one you see here.

SAY? (What did you say?)

This is usually signed with a frown, to indicate confusion or having missed what was just said.

UNDERSTAND

SORRY

This is different from apologizing; the nonmanual signals here show sympathy. The sign is also made at a slower pace.

EXCUSE ME

RIGHT (yes, right)

Also the sign for EXCUSE although the nonmanual signals differ.

This sign is usually accompanied by a nod.

SAME ME (*me, too, or same as me*).

The best things to do during a conversation with either a deaf or hearing person are to relax, be yourself, and let your personality show through!

HANDS-ON PRACTICE

Again, the best way to practice what you've learned in this hour is to actually interact with deaf people. Below are some suggested practice sentences. Try to find a fellow signer, preferably fluent, to practice with you.

Sign a sentence …

1. That includes the sign DEAF.
2. That shows you're confused.
3. Using a negation, and give the correct answer in response.
4. That tells where you went to school (name the school and location).
5. That asks if the other person went to a residential school.
6. That tells who you are to a group of deaf people.
7. Excusing yourself to go get a drink.
8. Telling how old your siblings (or children) are.
9. That uses the number 179.
10. That tells why you are learning ASL.

HOUR'S UP!

Here's a quiz to help you review some of the facts and ideas presented during this hour. Some questions have more than one answer. (You can find the correct answers in Appendix A.)

1. Why will a deaf person often ask if you're deaf or hearing?
    a. To see if you can interpret
    b. To identify your experiences within the deaf community
    c. To discuss hearing losses
    d. To see if you are fluent at ASL

2. True or False: It is appropriate to ask a deaf person about his level of hearing loss.

3. Typical information in a personal exchange includes …
    a. Educational background.
    b. Hearing loss.
    c. Family.
    d. Occupation.

4. You should ____ during a conversation to show you are following.
    a. Smile
    b. Do nothing
    c. Say "mm-mm"
    d. Nod

5. In the following figure, what is the signer showing?

    a. Remorse

    b. Anger

    c. Confusion

    d. Sympathy

6. True or False: The deaf person can probably identify if you're deaf or hearing, so it's not necessary to say whether you're deaf or hearing.

7. How should you tell the other person you don't understand?

    a. Nod.

    b. Push down his hands.

    c. Raise your hand at mid-chest and frown slightly.

    d. You don't tell him.

8. What type of setting did this signer grow up in?

    a. Residential school

    b. Mainstreamed program

    c. Oral program

    d. Charter school

9. If a deaf person says he grew up in an oral program, what implications does this have?

    a. He likely knew sign language all his life.

    b. He probably didn't learn sign language until later in life.

    c. He grew up having to speak orally in school.

    d. His family probably doesn't/didn't know sign language.

10. What is the signer saying in the following figure?

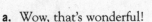

a. Wow, that's wonderful!

b. Wow, that's bad.

c. Really? That's so good!

d. Really? That's sad.

VOCABULARY

Here's a summary of the signs you've learned in this hour:

COLLEGE	DEAF SCHOOL (*residential school*)
ELEMENTARY	EXCUSE-ME
FORGET	GOOD
GRADUATION	GROW-UP
HIGH SCHOOL	INTERPRETER
LEARN	MAINSTREAMED
ORAL	REALLY?
RIGHT (*Yes, right*)	SAME-ME (*Me, too*)
SCHOOL	SORRY
STUDENT	UNDERSTAND
UNIVERSITY	WANT
WHAT-SAY?	WOW
YOU BORN DEAF?	

RECAP

In this hour, you learned about conversational indicators, personal exchange of information, and why you might be asked if you're deaf or hearing. In the next hour, you'll talk about and learn the signs for family ties.

HOUR 11

Introducing Family and Friends

- Hearing households with a deaf child.
- Why Deaf people celebrate the birth of a deaf child.
- Options for hearing parents to include deaf children.
- Family-related signs.

All of us have been influenced by our family experiences. We learn values, social skills, and other life-altering details from our family and friends.

For a deaf person, the biggest influences in his life usually are his or her parents. They decide at an early age what communication method the deaf child will use, how the child will learn English, and what educational options will be pursued. The choices aren't always successful or the best, but parents always have good intentions; they want what is best for their child.

Unfortunately, when the choices turn out to have unintended results, the deaf person might grow up to resent his parents. Many of us resent our parents, deaf or not, but a deaf person may become somewhat alienated from his family due to communication barriers. This resentment or disappointment is heightened even more if the deaf person uses sign language, but his parents do not accept the use of ASL.

FAMILY TIES

Many deaf people tell of how they felt left out or excluded at the dinner table or at family gatherings, or even during a night of watching TV with siblings and parents. They might have asked what was said, but often would be told, "Never mind, it's not that important." Or maybe everyone would be laughing, and the deaf person wouldn't be because he didn't understand what was said.

Edna Johnston of Columbia College's ASL-English Interpretation Department in Chicago did an informal study on growing up with hearing families, talking with 15 deaf adults who were either frustrated with their hearing parents or felt distant from their parents. The participants remembered some activities that helped to minimize their being excluded were playing board games (this is also ideal for family gatherings with deaf adults present), having pets (the deaf and hearing children could both play with the pets), playing sports, or watching captioned television. It is also interesting to note that 12 out of the 15 interviewed adults recommend that parents learn ASL.

This sense of being left out is one reason why deaf people sometimes prefer the company of other deaf people rather than their own hearing family—communication is available and accessible, and they can decide for themselves what is important. They also won't be criticized for their deafness and life choices. They realize that their family and parents love them, but they want to be able to express themselves instead of having to struggle. It's usually easier for a hearing person to learn sign language than a deaf person to learn to speak.

Many deaf people who attended residential schools tell of how they hated going home on weekends or for holidays for this same reason; they were put back in a situation where there was little or limited communication (and became more delayed in their language development). They often counted the days until they could return to the school, where they had access to communication with peers and role models 24 hours a day.

FYI Martha's Vineyard, Massachusetts, holds a special place in deaf history. For many decades, there was a high incidence of deaf births, mostly to hearing parents. An interesting result developed: Everyone on the island signed, regardless of whether they were deaf or hearing. Hearing people would sign with each other. Although this is no longer the case today, it reflects a time and place in history when deaf people were truly equals in a mixed community.

Often, when a deaf person finds out someone else is from a deaf family (meaning, that person's parents and possibly siblings are deaf), he might say, "You're so lucky!" What this represents is an acknowledgment that the deaf person grew up in a household that had no communication barriers or exclusion, and that the deaf person had ASL (usually) as his first language.

This access to language and culture is why Deaf people often celebrate the birth of a deaf baby to deaf parents. *The Washington Post* printed a controversial story in April 2002 about a deaf lesbian couple that had specifically received sperm donation from a deaf man who had a history of deaf genes in his family. Many hearing people were furious over the couple's actions, saying that the deaf parents were intentionally disabling their baby (who, unfortunately, died a short time later from unrelated causes) and that culturally deaf people were in "deep denial" of their disability.

These hearing people obviously did not realize or accept that ASL is a language and that Deaf people actually have a culture. The desire that drives hearing parents to have their children learn the same language and values is the same desire deaf parents have for their children. And don't forget—Deaf people don't consider themselves disabled. Rather, they are a cultural entity.

When a deaf baby is born—to either hearing or deaf parents—it means the deaf community has a new member, and this is cause for celebration for some Deaf people. Deaf people look at it this way: The deaf child will be introduced to a culture with a rich history and language. The language and community's close-knit nature easily outweigh the frustrations and discrimination experienced.

Today, there are many organizations and support groups that provide information on language choice, communication methods, and educational rights for the parents of deaf children. One such organization is the American Society of Deaf Children (www.deafchildren.org).

GENDER-ORIENTED SIGNS

When you look at the following signs, you might notice one characteristic: Female signs are made in the bottom half of the face, and male signs are on the top half. This is similar to the –o and –a endings in Spanish signifying male and female.

One possible explanation for this is that during the 1800s, males wore hats, while females wore bonnets. Most signs other than the ones listed with the following figures do not indicate gender, because the gender is often identified by other words in the sentence.

MOTHER

FATHER

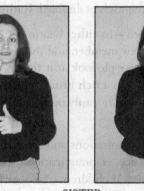

SISTER

There are many variations of this sign, but this is the most commonly used one.

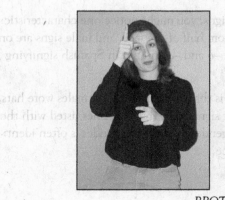

BROTHER

There are many variations of this sign, but this is the most commonly used one.

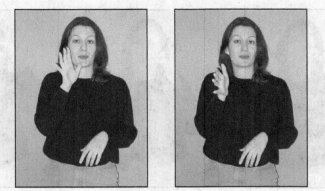

GRANDMOTHER

Bounce the hand away from the chin. Some bounce the 5 hand-shape twice in the air; however, one bounce is acceptable.

GRANDFATHER

Bounce the hand away from the forehead. Some bounce the 5 handshape twice in the air; however, one bounce is acceptable.

AUNT   UNCLE

COUSIN

Shake the C handshape slightly.

NIECE

Shake the N handshape slightly on the side of the chin.

NEPHEW

Shake the N handshape slightly on the side of the forehead.

DAUGHTER

This has evolved from the signs for GIRL and BABY.

SON

This has evolved from the signs for BOY and BABY.

WIFE

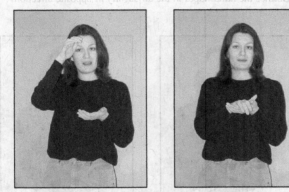

HUSBAND

PARTNER (also the sign for SHARE)

BABY

CHILD (signed with one hand)

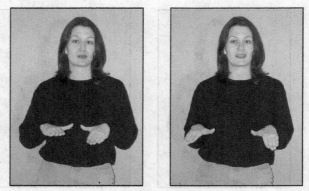

CHILDREN

Bounce the handshapes in the air slightly in opposite directions.

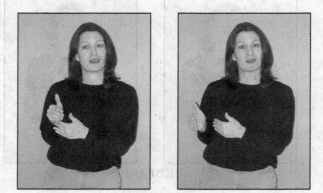

NEIGHBOR

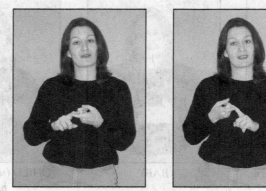

FRIEND (*acquaintance*)

FRIEND (close or good friend)

BEST FRIEND

Move intertwined index fingers straight down.

BEST FRIEND

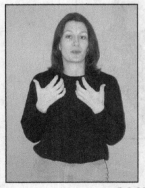

ROOMMATE

Repeat motion.

GIRL

Move thumb slightly down on the cheek.

BOY

WOMAN

MAN

DATING
Move the hands, staying in
this position, back and forth
in repeated motions.

DATING
This is another commonly
used sign; it signifies seriously dating or going steady.

GIRLFRIEND
BOYFRIEND is signed the same way, with BOY in lieu of GIRL.

MARRY (married)
Notice this is similar to HUSBAND and WIFE,
without any gender indication.

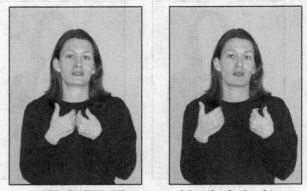

SEPARATED *(She's separated from her husband.)*

DIVORCED

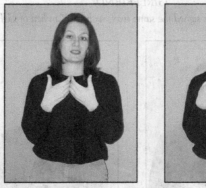

DIVORCED

Although the version shown previously is more common,
this version is also common.

SINGLE (*No, he's single.*)   SINGLE (*I'm single.*)

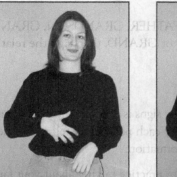

PREGNANT
The handshape moves out, showing a swollen belly.

BORN

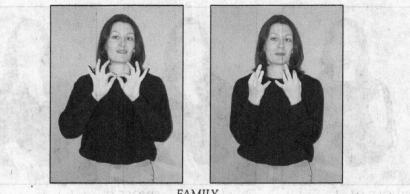

FAMILY

Move the F handshape around in a circle.

For STEPMOTHER, STEPFATHER, GRANDSON, GRANDDAUGHTER, and so on, fingerspell STEP or GRAND, then sign the relation.

HANDS-ON PRACTICE

A great way to practice family signs is to look at family pictures or pictures of you with your friends. Identify each person and tell about their educations, ages, and other relevant information.

Another excellent method to practice talking about your family is to draw a family tree. The following figure gives you a sample for practice. Identify each relative, and sign their names and the years they were born. Then when you finish, create your own family tree.

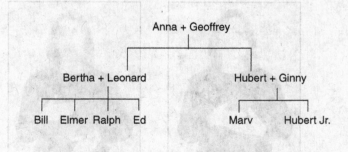

Hour's Up!

Here's a quiz to help you review some of the facts and ideas presented during this hour. Some questions have more than one answer. (You can find the correct answers in Appendix A.)

1. Students at residential schools for the deaf often may not want to go home during extended vacations because ...

   a. They want to be with their friends at school.

   b. They often feel left out at home with their hearing families.

   c. Communication is often not available at home.

   d. Everyone can sign with the deaf child.

2. A hearing family can try to include a deaf child by ...

   a. Playing board games.

   b. Insisting the child learn how to speak.

   c. Getting a pet for all the siblings and parents to play with.

   d. Encouraging the child to practice lipreading.

3. True or False: Deaf people often celebrate when Deaf parents give birth to a deaf baby.

4. Martha's Vineyard was unique in that ...

   a. Hearing and deaf people stayed completely segregated.

   b. Hearing people knew ASL and deaf people did not.

   c. Deaf people knew ASL and hearing people did not.

   d. Both hearing and deaf people used ASL.

5. What is the signer saying?

a. My sister is hearing.

b. My sister is deaf.

c. My brother is hearing.

d. My brother is deaf.

6. For family signs, male signs are located at ...

a. The forehead.

b. The side of the face.

c. The nose.

d. The chin.

7. One possible explanation for the gender-oriented signs is that ...

a. Males are smarter than females, so male words are signed at the forehead.

b. Males wore hats and females wore bonnets, so words are signed at the forehead and chin, respectively.

c. Females wear lipstick, so their signs are at the chin.

d. There is no explanation; it simply evolved that way.

8. What is the signer saying?

    a. My grandparents are separated.

    b. My grandparents are divorced.

    c. My parents are separated.

    d. My parents are divorced.

9. Why do deaf people often feel left out in hearing households?

    a. Nobody signs.

    b. When asking why everyone is laughing, deaf people are often told, "Never mind, it's not important."

    c. They're not deaf.

    d. There's nothing to do.

10. True or False: It's harder for a hearing person to learn ASL than a deaf person to learn how to speak.

Vocabulary List

Here's a summary of the signs you've learned in this hour:

AUNT	BABY
BEST FRIEND	BORN
BOY	BROTHER
CHILD	CHILDREN
COUSIN	DATING
DAUGHTER	DIVORCED
FAMILY	FATHER
FRIEND (*acquaintance*)	FRIEND (*close/good*)
GIRL	GIRL/BOYFRIEND
GRANDFATHER	GRANDMOTHER
GRANDSON (*granddaughter, grandniece, and so on*)	HUSBAND
MAN	MARRY
MOTHER	NEIGHBOR
NEPHEW	NIECE
PARTNER	PREGNANT

ROOMMATE   SEPARATED
SINGLE   SISTER
SON   STEPMOTHER (*stepfather*)
UNCLE   WIFE
WOMAN

RECAP

In this hour, you learned about some family dynamics that might affect how a deaf person feels about being around his hearing family members who do not sign or sign very little. You also learned various signs for family members and friends. In the next hour, you'll look at locations and surroundings.

HOUR 12

Talking About Locations

CHAPTER SUMMARY

LESSON PLAN:

In this hour, you'll learn about signing ...

- Types of residences.
- Cities.
- States.

When you chat with a deaf person, the conversation will naturally turn to where you live or have lived. This is a great conversational topic for anyone, hearing or deaf. In the Deaf community, locations are especially important, because of the close-knit nature of the community.

Deaf people usually know other deaf people from all parts of the country, especially if they've attended Gallaudet, CSUN, or NTID—or if they attended residential schools. Residential schools often participate in multi-state tournaments, where residential schools from various states come together to compete. Also, deaf people often travel great distances to attend deaf gatherings, and these gatherings are where they meet people from all over the country.

Chances are that when you tell a deaf person where you're from, the person will start asking you if you know someone in your geographical area. This is part of the ways deaf people try to form friendships (as I discussed in Hour 9)—by identifying shared experiences and/or acquaintances.

TELLING WHERE YOU LIVE

Once again, the signs for your towns or landmarks might be local, so rather than give you very specific signs, I'll give you the most commonly used signs. If you want to know local signs, the best bet is to ask native signers or longtime members of the Deaf community who live in your area.

LIVE

Bring the hands up slightly on your chest.

HOME

This sign has evolved from EAT and BED.

NEAR

Note how proximity is expressed by nonmanual signals.

NEAR

Mostly used by fluent signers, this shows extremely close proximity.

FAR

This is the more commonly used of two versions.

FAR

This is the less-used version.

RENT

The other, more common, way is to fingerspell the word rent.
The sign shown here is similar to MONTH, but is made with
repeated and quicker movements.

ROOM

Signed as if showing four walls.

STREET *(can also be used for ROAD)*

CITY (or TOWN)
Repeat the motion twice.

The following words are fingerspelled:

APT (apartment)   RENT
CONDO   T-H (townhouse)
AVE (avenue)   BLVD (boulevard)
LANE

GEOGRAPHICAL SIGNS

There are not signs for every state or city. Some are fingerspelled; others have actual signs, and I've categorized these in this section. Some states that are fingerspelled do have their own in-state signs, but I've chosen to show you the most commonly used versions.

FYI Some city name signs come from curious beginnings. The sign for Minneapolis comes from the name sign of a resident named Dean. His name sign was a D on the shoulder. His friends would often say, "Let's go visit Dean," and the name sign evolved into the city sign. The same is true for San Antonio, Texas—except the man had a name that started with G. Although there are several versions of the story that explains why San Antonio is signed this way, this is the one believed to be most accurate.

MAJOR CITIES

Let's start with the cities.

ATLANTA

Start at the opposite shoulder, and bring it over to the other shoulder.

BALTIMORE

Bounce the B in the air twice.

BOSTON

This sign is very similar to BALTIMORE with different palm orientation. Bounce the handshape twice.

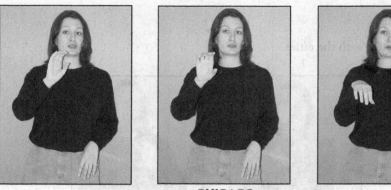

CHICAGO

Bring the C over and down in a smooth motion.

The old sign for Chicago was waving C in the air, staying in one location; it has evolved into this modern version.

CLEVELAND

This sign is similar to ATLANTA.

DENVER

Wave the D in the air slightly.

DETROIT

This sign is similar to CHICAGO, with a different handshape.

HOUSTON

Bounce the H on your chin twice.

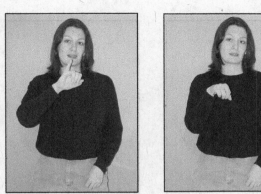

INDIANAPOLIS

This sign is also similar to CHICAGO, with a different handshape.

MILWAUKEE

This sign is made with repeated motions.

MINNEAPOLIS

Use a D handshape, bouncing it slightly on the shoulder opposite your dominant hand.

NEW ORLEANS

Repeat this motion twice.

NEW YORK CITY

Another way is to simply fingerspell NYC.

PHILADELPHIA

This sign is similar to CHICAGO, with a different handshape.

PHOENIX

Similar to DENVER with an X handshape.

PITTSBURGH

Repeat the small circular motion on the shoulder nearest your dominant hand.

SEATTLE

This sign is similar to DENVER with an S handshape.

WASHINGTON D.C.

The sign for WASHINGTON is formed, then D.C. is fingerspelled

Other fingerspelled cities include ...

KC (Kansas City)

DALLAS (Another sign, usually used by Texans, is to form a D at the forehead)

LA (Los Angeles; also the sign for LOUISIANA)

SF (San Francisco)

STATES

The following figures show you how to sign states.

ARIZONA

*Start at the cheek opposite your dominant hand, then bring
the A over to the other cheek.*

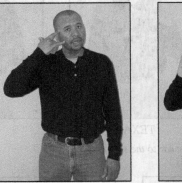

CALIFORNIA

This sign is also the sign for GOLD; stems from the Gold Rush.

WASHINGTON

Bring the W out from your shoulder.

NEW YORK

This sign can also be used to sign New York City.

TEXAS

This sign is similar to the sign for CHICAGO.

WEST VA

WEST is signed first, then VA is fingerspelled.

You'll sometimes have to use the words North, South, East, or West. They're signed much as they're shown on a compass:

NORTH   SOUTH   WEST

If your dominant hand is your left hand, you will sign WEST without flipping the hand as shown here, and flip the hand for EAST instead.

EAST

If you want to sign words like northwest or southeast, sign SOUTH then EAST in a fluid motion.

The following states are fingerspelled, but abbreviated. Note that postal abbreviations are not used.

ALA (Alabama)   ARK (Arkansas)

COLO (Colorado)   CONN (Connecticut)

FLA (Florida)	GA (Georgia)
ILL (Illinois)	IND (Indiana)
KAN (Kansas)	KY (Kentucky)
LA (Louisiana; this is similar to Los Angeles)	MD (Maryland)
	MINN (Minnesota)
MASS (Massachusetts)	NC (North Carolina)
MICH (Michigan)	NEB (Nebraska)
MO (Missouri)	NH (New Hampshire)
ND (North Dakota)	NM (New Mexico)
NEV (Nevada)	PA (Pennsylvania)
NJ (New Jersey)	SC (South Carolina)
OKLA (Oklahoma)	TENN (Tennessee)
RI (Rhode Island)	WISC (Wisconsin; Wisconsin natives tend to fingerspell WIS without the C, but WISC is the common version)
SD (South Dakota)	
VA (Virginia)	

The following states are fingerspelled with no abbreviations:

ALASKA	HAWAII
IDAHO	IOWA
MAINE	MISSISSIPPI
MONTANA	OHIO
OREGON	UTAH
WYOMING	

HANDS-ON PRACTICE

Practice with a friend, and tell each other about people you know. Include names, ages, educational background, where people live, and types of housing. This is a good opportunity to practice your fingerspelling and use new signs and numbers. Here is a sample narrative:

My friend, John, is 36 and was born in Detroit. He grew up in Chicago, and moved to a suburb near Tampa, Florida, when he got married. He has three children, ages 10, 7, and 2. He lives in a big house with 14 rooms.

Remember to incorporate nonmanual signals, ASL grammatical rules, and register in your ASL. For example, in ASL, the previous narrative might be signed like this:

FRIEND NAME JOHN AGE-36, HE (point) BORN DETROIT. GROW-UP CHICAGO, GOT MARRY, MOVE FLORIDA, NEAR TAMPA WEST. HE HAVE CHILDREN 3 HOW OLD? (rhetorical question) AGE 10, 7, 2. NOW LIVE HOUSE BIG, HAVE 14 ROOM.

Practice with addresses, cities, and states, and even ZIP codes. The phone book is another a handy resource in this exercise. Alternatively, you can also …

- Open up an atlas or a map of the United States. Sign or fingerspell random locations, and make up stories about characters who live in specific cities. Be creative!
- Look in the newspaper's real estate section. Find pictures of different types of housing, look at ads, and sign the prices, rental costs, and locations.

HOUR'S UP!

Here's a quiz to help you review some of the facts and ideas presented during this Hour. (You can find the correct answers in Appendix A.)

1. Identify the location:

   a. Minneapolis

   b. Washington, D.C.

   c. Pittsburgh

   d. Milwaukee

2. Identify the location:

a. Washington, D.C.

b. Phoenix

c. Denver

d. Seattle

3. True or False: To identify states, you should use the postal abbreviation.

4. Identify the location:

a. Chicago

b. Indianapolis

c. Texas

d. Detroit

5. True or False: Some states have their own in-state signs.

6. When someone asks where you are from, you should ...

    a. Use the local sign for the town or state.

    b. Fingerspell the town and street address.

    c. Say the state or, if appropriate, fingerspell the town.

    d. Give the street address, town, and state.

7. Name the state being fingerspelled:

    a. Minnesota

    b. Texas

    c. Nebraska

    d. Tennessee

8. Name the state being fingerspelled:

    a. Alabama

    b. Florida

    c. Oklahoma

    d. Indiana

9. The signer lives …

a. In an apartment with her father.

b. In a house with her mother.

c. In her father's townhouse.

d. In her mother's townhouse.

10. The signer lives on …

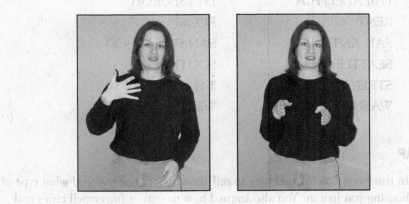

a. 3rd Street.

b. 4th Street.

c. 5th Street.

d. 6th Street.

VOCABULARY LIST

Here's a summary of the signs you've learned in this hour:

50 STATES	APT
ATLANTA	AVE
BALTIMORE	BLVD
BOSTON	CHICAGO
CITY/TOWN	CLEVELAND
CONDO	DALLAS
DENVER	DETROIT
EAST	FAR
HOME	HOUSTON

INDIANAPOLIS   KANSAS CITY
LANE   LIVE
MILWAUKEE   MINNEAPOLIS
NEAR   NEW ORLEANS
NEW YORK CITY   NORTH
PHILADELPHIA   PITTSBURGH
RENT   ROOM
SAN ANTONIO   SAN FRANCISCO
SEATTLE   SOUTH
STREET   T-H
WASHINGTON, D.C.   WEST

RECAP

In this hour, you learned how to tell about where you live and what type of housing you live in. You also learned how to sign or fingerspell cities and states. In the next hour, you'll move onto classifiers.

PART IV

Being Descriptive

Part IV
Being Descriptive

HOUR 13

Using Classifiers

LESSON PLAN:

In this hour, you'll learn about ...

- Different classifier hand-shapes.
- The role of location and eye gaze.
- Showing movement using classifiers.

By now you've learned how nonmanual signals and grammar are essential to ASL. Another important aspect of ASL is the use of classifiers.

WHAT ARE CLASSIFIERS?

ASL has various handshapes that represent movement, placement, and visual characteristics (such as texture or size) of a person or object. These handshapes are known as *classifiers*. This is one of the major differences between ASL and English. Although many other spoken languages use other forms of classifiers, English has very few (an example is "school of fish" or "herd of cattle").

The best way to understand what a classifier does in ASL is to see it in action. The following figures present a list of different signs all using the 2 handshape. Notice that the handshape stays the same, but the movement, palm orientation, and location differ. Nonmanual signals also can make the same sign different in meaning.

A person standing.

Two people walking by.

A person laying down.

A person watching something.

A person looking up.

A person reading.

In the previous examples, one handshape is used with at least six meanings with different movements and locations. Each classifier handshape has multiple uses. If you look back at all the signs you've learned up to this point, you'll see the same handshapes used over and over in different ways.

Classifiers in ASL are used to demonstrate nouns and pronouns, objects, animals, persons, vehicles, size, shape, depth, and texture. They're also used to demonstrate perspectives, adverbs, and verbs.

CLASSIFIER HANDSHAPES

Each classifier handshape has a specific movement, location, and shape. We'll look at only a sampling of the handshapes that are commonly used, although there are many more. Below each picture is a list of some words that use this handshape, with the sign pictured indicated in capital letters.

1

Person, PENCIL, pole.

2

Stand, two people, LOOK AT EACH OTHER.

3

Car, PARKED VEHICLES, three people. (Note: The 3 handshape usually represents vehicles with wheels—such as cars, bicycles, trucks, motorcycles, and buses.)

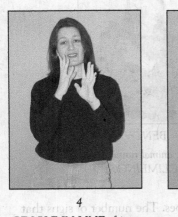

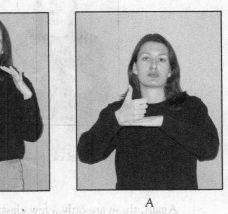

4

PEOPLE IN LINE, *fringes, water running. (Note: The nonmanual signals show that the line is long.)*

5

Pile, CROWD, waves.

A

Person, jar, SOMETHING ON A SHELF. (Note: The A handshape is often used to show things set up on a surface, such as jars on a shelf or bottles on a table.)

B

Door, PLATFORM, *flat surfaces*.

C

Can, thick (book), POUR.

F

Coin, peephole, WRIST-WATCH.

L

PLATE, clock, big-shouldered.

BENT-V

Sit, *animal running,* CLIMBING.

Again, these are only a few classifier handshapes. The number of signs that use these handshapes are in the hundreds. Another important aspect of using classifiers is locatives.

LOCATIVES

Classifiers also can differ in meaning by location. Usually, when a signer describes something or narrates an event, his or her eye gaze will follow the actual events or locations. As mentioned earlier, eye gaze plays an important role in ASL. If a signer is telling about how he bumped into a tall man, he will look up as if he is actually looking at the man.

ME   BUMP

MAN   TALL

But if he talks about how he bumped into a child, his eye gaze will move downward to demonstrate height. Note his use of the 1 handshape to indicate two people, and his nonmanual signals.

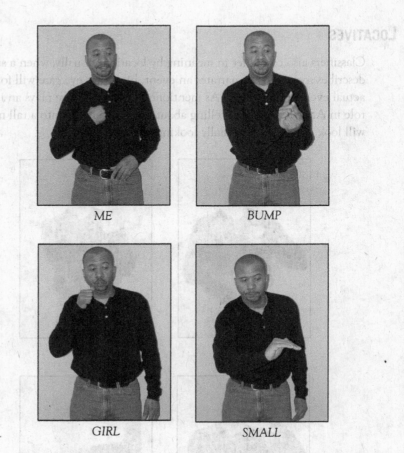

ME

BUMP

GIRL

SMALL

The nonmanual signals you use change the meanings of the classifiers. If the signer had frowned as he signed "bumped," that would mean it was not a pleasant encounter or maybe someone got hurt in the accidental encounter. If he showed a look of surprise with a smile, obviously it was a pleasant encounter.

Another example is where something is located. If a signer tells about where he placed a flowerpot in his house, his eye gaze will follow the hand location. If the flowerpot is placed on a low end table, his eye gaze will lower as he shows the "lower" location of the flowerpot (with his hand lowered also), or if it's placed on a window ledge, his eye gaze will be slightly higher in tune with the higher hand placement.

MOVEMENT

Movement is also essential in the use of classifiers, which can be illustrated by using the ocean for an example. Here, the signer uses the 5 handshape to show the water.

Calm water.

Big waves.

Rising water.

Note how he shows the calmness of the water with his lips and calm facial expression, then shows the bigger waves with puffed cheeks and a frown. Also, his eye gaze follows the location of the water. If he had used the same facial expression from the first example, you would have known that the waves were calm and not so big.

FYI If you'd like more practice on using classifiers, you can check out this excellent videotape—the only one of its kind: *Pursuit of ASL: Interesting Facts Using Classifiers*, with Angela Petrone Stratiy (who is deaf). The tape offers 35 passages of useful facts and tips. The videotape, however, is not voiced over in English. You can purchase it at www.aslinterpreting.com/content/tapes.htm.

Classifiers are essential to ASL in showing the quality and size of something, and to demonstrate actions. As you read through the book, always be conscious of handshapes and their locations or movements.

HANDS-ON PRACTICE

Look in your kitchen pantry or refrigerator, or any room in your house. Use classifiers to describe the different objects' shapes and locations. You can do this with a friend: Choose an item and have the other person guess which item you are describing.

HOUR'S UP!

Here's a quiz to help you review some of the facts and ideas presented during this hour. Match the item you think most fits the signer's descriptions. Be sure to look at the shape that the hands make. (You can find the correct answers in Appendix A.)

1. Classifiers are …

    a. Nonmanual signals that represent movement, placement, and visual characteristics of a person or object.

    b. Nonmanual signals that represent movement, placement, and visual characteristics of an action.

    c. Handshapes that represent movement, placement, and visual characteristics of a person or object.

    d. Handshapes that represent movement, placement, and visual characteristics of an action.

2. True or False: A, B, C, F, and V are all examples of classifier handshapes.

3. True or False: Nonmanual signals can change a classifier's meaning, even if the sign remains the same.

4. Match the item you think best fits the signer's descriptions.

5.

6.

3. True or False: Nonmanual signals can change a classifier, meaning, even if the sign remains the same.

4. Match the item you think best fits the descriptions.

7.

8.

9.

10.

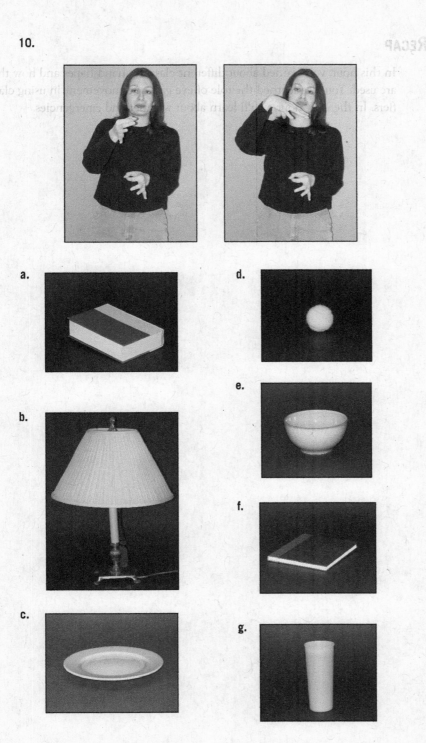

RECAP

In this hour, you learned about different classifier handshapes and how they are used. You also learned the role of eye gaze and movement in using classifiers. In the next hour, you'll learn about weather and emergencies.

HOUR 14

Talking About Weather and Emergencies

- Dangers of weather and emergencies.
- Communication barriers.
- Seasons.
- Weather types.
- Emergencies.

Weather and emergencies have always been a source of concern for people, hearing or deaf. Imagine having no access to weather information on television, having no access to emergency radio broadcasts, and no access to information that could very well be the factor between life and death. This is a dangerous reality the Deaf community has lived with for centuries. Fortunately, within the past 20 years—thanks to the advent of technology and a lot of advocacy—emergency information has become more accessible to deaf and hard of hearing people.

THE DANGERS OF WEATHER AND EMERGENCIES

During the tragedies of September 11, 2001, many cell phones and phone lines were nonoperational, but two-way pagers were in full operation and they were a blessing for many deaf people. These same people sent messages to family and friends even as they were running from the collapse of the World Trade Center. All the national television networks captioned the coverage of the tragedies almost nonstop, as well, which was a key resource for deaf people tuning in to see what was happening.

FYI A deaf man who worked on the 105th floor of the World Trade Center was killed in the terrorist attacks of September 11, 2001. Many other deaf survivors were able to escape in time, and were profiled in various media outlets, including *Dateline* NBC. Almost all of the featured survivors credited their survival to their two-way pagers.

The accessibility to information that fateful day was a major improvement over past tragedies. Even so, there are still improvements to be made. In many rural areas, local news broadcasts aren't captioned or are only partially captioned. Live broadcasts, even in major cities, aren't always captioned. Oftentimes emergency weather notices scrolling across the bottom of televisions will distort or block closed captions. Closed-captioning companies and the Federal Communications Commission have been working closely with networks on overcoming these obstacles.

Many 9-1-1 centers are also notorious for hanging up on TTY or relay calls, mistakenly believing they're prank or telemarketing calls—even if they've been trained in responding to these types of calls. In Illinois, a deaf man's baby died after repeated attempts to call 9-1-1 on a TTY were ignored by the call center. Relay services, local agencies, deaf advocates, and emergency services have been working on this issue for many years.

Communication Barriers

Another dangerous barrier deaf people face in emergencies is the communication methods used. Emergency personnel or police often assume communicating via paper and pen is acceptable for situations involving a deaf victim or criminal or a seriously injured deaf person.

This is a potentially fatal assumption, because the deaf person might be too upset to write in English (especially if ASL is his first language), or might be too sick or injured to write. Plus, those makeshift communication methods do not give the deaf person equal access to communication, such as what is being said in background conversations, or full language access. The opportunity for miscommunication is too great if written communication is the sole method.

Emergency personnel also often believe lip reading is another acceptable communication method; even if the deaf person might say yes when asked if lip reading is a good way to communicate, it's still too dangerous. Remember, only a very small fraction of what is speechread is accurate; the rest is guesswork on the deaf person's part.

Even more dangerous is the use of unqualified and uncertified interpreters to translate. Although people (including emergency personnel) might have minimal or fluent knowledge of ASL, this does not qualify them to be interpreters in these situations. Unfortunately, many signers feel they know sufficient signs to "help out" in emergency situations without realizing that simply knowing sign language does not allow for smoother communication. More often than not, an unqualified signer/interpreter might worsen the situation.

FYI A police training program provided a six-week ASL course to approximately 50 of its officers in hopes that relations would improve between the police community and the Deaf community. A year later, only one officer remembered any of the signs. None of the officers had used the signs on a regular basis, so the signs were forgotten. The program decided to focus instead on providing the police with training on deaf awareness and appropriate communication options such as hiring interpreters.

In several murder cases, charges were thrown out of court after it was proven that the interpreters mistakenly translated something. The Registry of Interpreters for the Deaf and the National Association of the Deaf have long worked on alleviating these issues by establishing standards and providing advocacy, in addition to maintaining certification.

Simple traffic stops can also be stressful for deaf people, especially if the police officer is not trained in or sensitive to communication issues. In these situations, writing back and forth *might* be accepted. But more important is the police officer's understanding of the communication process, more so when the deaf person requests appropriate communication methods. There have been many situations where a police officer refused to give paper and pen to a deaf person, or even insisted on talking out of the deaf person's sightline. Training is key, though the high turnover rate of emergency personnel is yet another obstacle.

In an event of a terrorist attack or catastrophic weather—for instance, a tornado—if deaf people take shelter in a basement, chances are likely they won't have access to a radio, outside communication, or other essential emergency broadcasts. In these events, it's wise to set up some type of emergency plan with emergency personnel.

Until then, education and advocacy will need to continue, and hopefully emergency response will continue to improve for deaf people—especially with the increased use of two-way pagers and captioning.

WEATHER

A great conversational topic is, of course, the weather. What else controls our activities and lives so much? So let's learn the signs for the ever-changing weather.

SPRING

This sign is similar to the sign for grow; repeat the motion.

SUMMER

Repeat the motion.

FALL

Swat the elbow using a B handshape twice.

WINTER

There are several versions; a common version is to use a W handshape.

HOT

Nonmanual signals can demonstrate the level of heat.

COLD

The signer almost "shivers" when signing COLD.

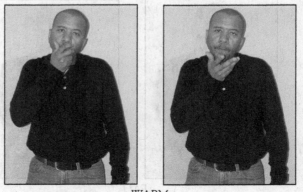

WARM

Unfold the hand while moving it up slightly.

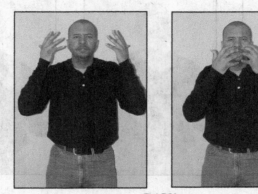

DARK

BRIGHT

RAIN
Repeat motion.

Nonmanual signals can show the intensity of weather. Take, for example, the various signs for RAIN. As you look at each of the following figures, notice the different variations on the same word, along with the different nonmanual signals.

RAIN (drizzle)
The OO mouth morpheme is used to show the light drizzle, and the hands move in small motions.

RAIN (heavy rain)
A frown, pursed lips, and slightly larger motions are used to show that the rain is heavy (but not torrential).

RAIN (torrential downpour)
Larger motions show the direction of the rain and intensity; the frown and puffed cheeks show the severity of the rain.

These different nonmanual signals can be applied to many different weather conditions: heat, cold, snow, thunder, and so on.

PROCEED WITH CAUTION

RAIN and SNOW are often confused; be sure to distinguish these clearly. RAIN is signed with bent fingers, while SNOW uses wiggling fingers.

SNOW

Wiggle the fingers as hands are brought down.

FREEZE

ICE/ICY is fingerspelled.

WINDY

Sway hands back and forth as shown in figure to illustrate wind blowing.

CLOUDY

Move hands across the air in a circular motion. There are also a few variations on handshape, but generally, both hands are used in a circular motion.

THUNDER

The mouth morpheme and motion show the "vibration" of thunder.

LIGHTNING

TORNADO

Move the hand across the space in front of your chest to show a moving tornado, as your fingers make circles opposite each other.

HURRICANE

This seems to be the most common version, although there are several variations.

DROUGHT (DRY)

This sign is similar to SUMMER, but it's made in one motion instead of repeated, and on the chin. Notice the signer's facial expression: frowning and looking uncomfortable. DROUGHT is not a positive weather condition, so the nonmanual signals are appropriately negative.

WATER
Bounce the W on the lips.

WET

FLOOD

SUN

Sign WATER, then move hands up to show the rising of water.

A full C handshape is used to sign SUN, bouncing on the temple. To sign MOON, use the first or second two fingers of your hand in a C handshape and sign it the same way as SUN.

RAINBOW

Draw a rainbow in the air.

STAR

EMERGENCIES

Hopefully, you'll never need to use signs for emergencies, but it's probably a good idea to know these signs just in case. Remember, simply knowing these signs does not qualify you to interpret. Only a certified, qualified interpreter should do the interpreting in these situations.

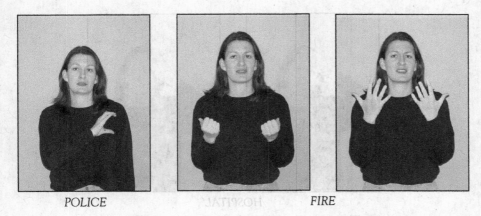

POLICE   FIRE

To sign FIRE DEPT, first sign FIRE, then fingerspell DEPT. For FIREMAN, there are several versions; I'll show you two.

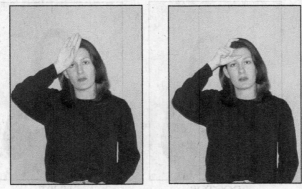

These are the two versions of FIREMAN

HOSPITAL

Make a small cross on the opposite shoulder using the first two fingers of the dominant hand.

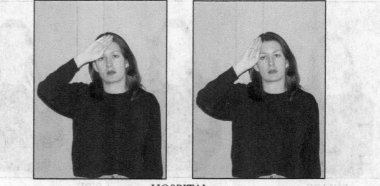

HOSPITAL

This version is mostly used in the eastern United States.

DOCTOR

Signers use a D or M hand-shape or a full hand to sign this word; NURSE is signed the same way, with an N handshape.

HURT

Move the index fingers back and forth slightly.

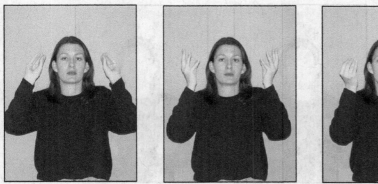

AMBULANCE

This sign shows sirens flashing.

ACCIDENT (*car accident*)

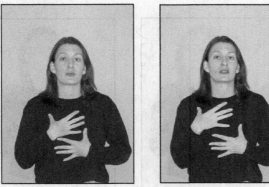

BREATHE

Bring hands out on the chest as if taking in a breath of air.

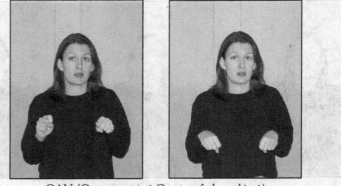

CAN (Can you move? Can you feel anything?)

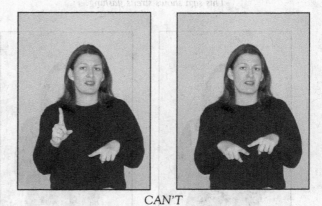

CAN'T

The dominant index finger is brought down on the other
index finger.

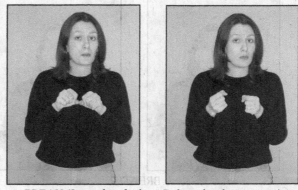

BREAK (Is anything broken? Did you break your arm?)

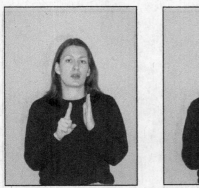

ALARM

CALL/PHONE

Bounce your index finger against the other hand twice.
To say FIRE ALARM, sign FIRE then ALARM.

HELP

Some people bounce the A handshape (as shown here); others
keep the A handshape stationary on the B handshape, and
bring both hands up slightly.

LOST (*I'm lost; I've lost my keys.*)

EMERGENCY

Shake both E handshapes in the air, although one hand can be used.

FIGHT (physical)

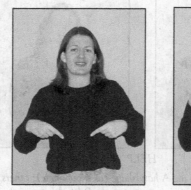

FIGHT (verbal; one of two ways to sign this)

FIGHT (verbal; one of two ways to sign this)

CAR   BREAK-DOWN

TIRE FLAT (fingerspell TIRE, then sign FLAT)

RAPE

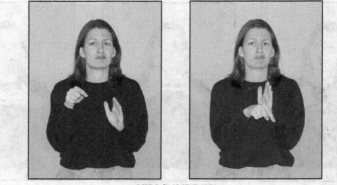

KILL/MURDER

HANDS-ON PRACTICE

Here are two exercises that help you practice what you've learned in this section:

- Read the weather report for different locations throughout the world online at www.weather.com or in the newspaper. Describe the different conditions and temperatures using signs.

- Read newspaper articles about accidents or incidents. Imagine you are the victim, the criminal or a witness, and describe the incident to a signing partner.

HOUR'S UP!

Here's a quiz to help you review some of the facts and ideas presented during this hour. Some of the questions have more than one answer. (You can find the correct answers in Appendix A.)

1. Deaf people often are at risk during weather emergencies because ...

    a. Emergency broadcasts are often not captioned.

    b. They do not hear radio broadcasts when taking shelter.

    c. They do not check for emergency information.

    d. Emergency personnel often do not include deaf people in emergency or safety plans.

2. Why do 9-1-1 operators often hang up on TTY or relay calls?

    a. Deaf people don't need emergency services.

    b. Deaf people should have hearing friends or relatives call for them.

    c. Operators think the calls are prank calls or telemarketers.

    d. Operators are not trained on these types of calls.

3. If you are part of an emergency with a deaf person, you should …

    a. Communicate as much as you can with the deaf person.

    b. Be the interpreter.

    c. Tell emergency personnel writing back and forth is acceptable.

    d. Do nothing.

4. When is writing back and forth usually not acceptable for a deaf individual?

    a. During criminal situations

    b. During emergency situations

    c. During simple traffic stops

    d. During hospital procedures

5. What has been a tremendous boost to deaf people's safety within the past few years?

    a. TTY services

    b. Relay services

    c. Emergency plans

    d. Two-way pagers

6. What's the emergency?

a. The woman's car had a flat tire.

b. The woman's car broke down.

c. The woman's house is on fire.

d. The woman's car is on fire.

7. How much is it raining?

a. Slightly

b. Moderately

c. Heavily

d. A downpour

8. What is the signer saying?

a. It's dark outside.

b. It's bright outside.

c. The moon is dark.

d. The sun is bright.

9. What's wrong with the girl?

a. She can't eat.

b. She can't see.

c. She can't breathe.

d. She can't drive.

10. What caused the car accident?

QUIZ

a. It was snowy, and I didn't see the car.

b. It was dark, and I didn't see the car.

c. It was wet, and I didn't see the pole.

d. It was snowy, and I didn't see the pole.

VOCABULARY LIST

Here's a summary of the signs you've learned in this hour:

ACCIDENT (*car*)	ALARM
AMBULANCE	BREAK (*arm*)
BREATHE	BRIGHT
CALL (*phone*)	CAN
CAN'T	CAR BREAK-DOWN
CLOUDY	COLD
DARK	DOCTOR
DROUGHT/DRY	EMERGENCY
FALL	FIGHT (*physical*)
FIGHT (*verbal*)	FIRE
FIRE DEPT	FIREMAN
FLOOD	FREEZE
HELP	HOSPITAL
HOT	HURRICANE
HURT	KILL

LIGHTNING	LOST
MOON	NURSE
POLICE	RAIN
RAINBOW	RAPE
SNOW	SPRING
STAR	SUMMER
SUN	THUNDER
TIRE FLAT	TORNADO
WARM	WATER
WET	WINDY
WINTER	

RECAP

In this hour, you learned about the problems deaf people face in events of bad weather or emergencies. You also read about how deaf people have struggled with access, and learned weather and emergency signs. In the next hour, you'll study signs for colors and adjectives.

HOUR 15

Using Colors and Adjectives

CHAPTER SUMMARY

LESSON PLAN:

In this hour, you'll learn about ...

- Colors.
- Adjectives.

Remember the general rule of thumb for adjective usage in ASL? They usually follow the words they describe. Although there are certainly various rules for adjective usage, for now follow this rule as we discuss colors and adjectives.

COLORS

Colors are used to describe many things, and they're usually used as an identifying detail in ASL. So let's quickly go through the colors. Note that most of them are repeated motions (that is, you make the sign twice in rapid succession).

RED

ORANGE

In this sign you "squeeze" an orange.

YELLOW

GREEN

This sign is similar to YEL-LOW, with a G handshape.

BLUE

This sign is similar to YEL-LOW, with a B handshape.

PURPLE

Shake the P handshape slightly.

PINK

This sign has evolved from a bent V on the lips.

BLACK

A singular motion.

WHITE

GRAY

This sign is similar to YEL-LOW, with a U handshape, although it is also signed with a R handshape. This word has several variations; most are regional.

GRAY

For this version of GRAY, move both hands back and forth over each other.

BROWN

Make a singular motion; repeated motions change the word to BEER.

TAN

This sign is similar to BROWN; this is also a singular motion.

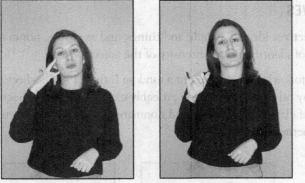

GOLD

This is similar to CALIFORNIA; the sign has evolved from
YELLOW + EARRING.

SILVER

This sign is similar to GOLD, with a S handshape.

COLOR

Wiggle your fingers on your
mouth.

If you'd like to describe a shade of blue that isn't just blue—such as baby blue or navy blue—you can describe it by using nonmanual signals and adding DARK or LIGHT.

ADJECTIVES

Adjectives identify people and things; and as always, nonmanual signals are part of identifying the intensity of the adjectives.

The following figures present a random listing of some adjectives. If you think of any other adjectives, you probably can describe the adjective through the use of classifiers, gestures, and nonmanual signals even when you don't know the actual signs.

PRETTY

UGLY

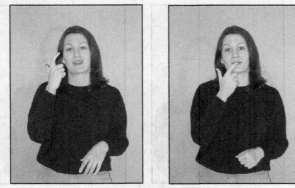

HANDSOME

Move the handshape back and forth over the face.

SMART

One of two versions.

SMART

This version isn't used as often as the previous version.

TALL

Remember that height
can be conveyed via
nonmanual signals.

SHORT (height-wise)

Again, nonmanual signals
can indicate just how short
someone is.

THIN

OVERWEIGHT

LAZY

Bounce the L on your
shoulder twice.

POLITE QUIET

This sign is similar to FINE; nonmanual signals distinguish the two words. Bounce the 5 handshape slightly on the chest.

FUNNY

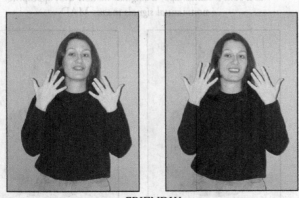

FRIENDLY

Move the hands back slightly in a singular motion.

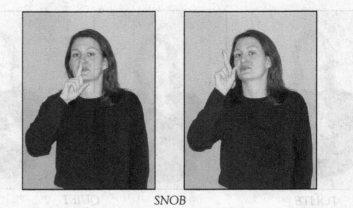

SNOB

The signer tilts her head up slightly while signing this, to illustrate snobbery (nose up in the air).

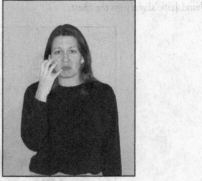

CRABBY

Repeat this motion with the handshape going from a 5 handshape to a bent 5 handshape; a singular motion with appropriate nonmanual signals means MAD.

NEW

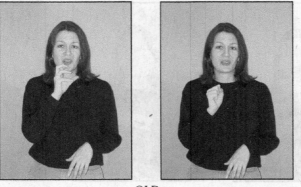

OLD

This is different from "How old?" Rather, this is used for sentences like, "The house is old," and is signed in a singular motion.

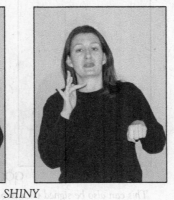

SHINY

SHARP

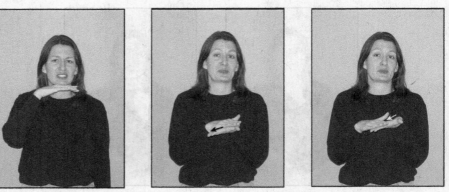

DIRTY   CLEAN

Wiggle fingers on chin.   *Similar to NICE; nonmanual signals distinguish the two signs.*

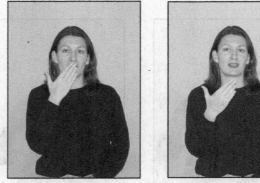

GOOD

This can also be signed with two hands, although it seems to be evolving to a one-handed sign.

BAD

This can also be signed with two hands, although it seems to be evolving to a one-handed sign.

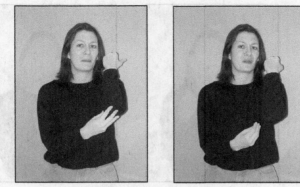

POOR *(differs from the sign for PITY/POOR)*

RICH

WEAK

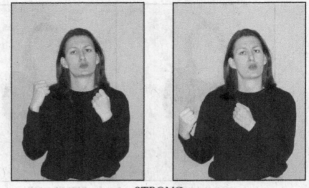

STRONG

Move your fists sideways slightly.

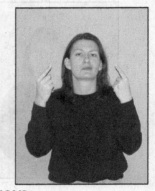

FAMOUS

This sign is similar to SUCCESS, which has different movements. Be cautious of the similarity.

STRANGE/ODD

NERVOUS

Make your hands tremble.

COURAGEOUS/BRAVE

AFRAID/FEARFUL

Move your hands back and forth toward each other.

STUBBORN

HANDS-ON PRACTICE

Here are two exercises to practice the words you just learned:

- Describe the texture, colors, and/or shapes of the following items:
  - Banana
  - Tree
  - Green and white striped tie
  - Old, beaten-up silver car with rust spots
  - Woman looking very afraid and wearing ratty clothes
  - Muddy, dirty floor
  - White house with green shutters and brick sidewalks

- 56-inch black television
- Silver spiral stairs
- Computer laptop
- Describe your house, family or friends, or things around you using the adjectives you've just learned.

HOUR'S UP!

Here's a quiz to help you review some of the facts and ideas presented during this hour. (You can find the correct answers in Appendix A.)

1. Which of the following would you use to describe a new car?

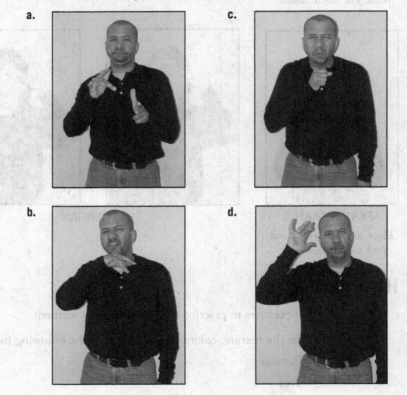

a.

b.

c.

d.

2. True or False: Nonmanual signals can show how intense an adjective is.

3. What color is the house?

    a. Pink and blue

    b. Red and blue

    c. Pink and brown

    d. Red and brown

4. What is the signer saying?

    a. The tall man is friendly.

    b. The tall boy is friendly.

    c. The tall man is crabby.

    d. The tall boy is crabby.

5. What color is the car?

   a. Black and white

   b. Pink and red

   c. Yellow and black

   d. White and yellow

6. What is the signer saying?

   a. The white floor is shiny.

   b. The green floor is shiny.

   c. The white floor is dirty.

   d. The green floor is dirty.

7. What is the signer saying?

a. My wife is smart.

b. My girlfriend is smart.

c. My wife is rich.

d. My girlfriend is rich.

8. How lazy is the boy?

a. Extremely lazy

b. Moderately lazy

c. Only a little lazy

d. Not lazy

9. What's wrong with the table?

a. The leg is broken.

b. The top is scratched.

c. The corner is sharp.

d. The table is old.

10. What is the signer saying about his two sisters?

QUIZ

a. One is a snob and the other is friendly.

b. One is funny and the other is quiet.

c. One is tall and the other is short.

d. One is crabby and the other is friendly.

VOCABULARY LIST

Here's a summary of the signs you've learned in this hour:

AFRAID/FEARFUL	BAD
BLACK	BLUE
BROWN	CLEAN
COLOR	COURAGEOUS/BRAVE
CRABBY	DIRTY
FAMOUS	FRIENDLY
FUNNY	GOLD
GOOD	GRAY
GREEN	HANDSOME
LAZY	NERVOUS
NEW	OLD
ORANGE	OVERWEIGHT
PINK	POLITE
POOR	PRETTY
PURPLE	QUIET

RED	RICH
SHARP	SHINY
SHORT	SILVER
SMART	SNOB
STRANGE/ODD	STRONG
STUBBORN	TALL
TAN	THIN
UGLY	WEAK
WHITE	YELLOW

RECAP

In this hour, you learned signs for colors and some adjectives. You also learned how nonmanual signals could change the intensity or meaning of an adjective. In the next hour, you'll learn how to identify things around the house.

HOUR 16

Moving Around the House

LESSON PLAN:

In this hour, you'll learn about ...

- Things in the house.
- Different rooms.
- Showing location.

For most of us, our homes are where we spend the majority of our time. It's also where we are hosts to family and friends. You'll probably talk about items or refer to specific rooms in your house during conversations, so it's a good idea to know the signs for these. Let's go room by room and look at common items or activities.

HOUSE

First, we'll look at signs that refer to the general structure of most homes.

DOORBELL

HOUSE

"Draw" a house.

DOOR

Repeat the motion; a singular motion is OPEN.

DOORBELL

"Push" a doorbell.

WALL

This is usually fingerspelled; however, if you're describing where to hang a picture or where to place a sofa, you'd sign it this way.

FLOOR

"Lay out" a floor.

STAIRS

This sign looks like legs climbing stairs. Directionality is important here. If you are going upstairs, move the hand upward; if you're going downstairs, move the hand downward.

WINDOW

UPSTAIRS

Point upstairs; repeat the motion.

DOWNSTAIRS

Point downstairs; repeat the motion.

The following words are fingerspelled:

ATTIC   ROOF

LIVING ROOM

Now let's look at furniture and items within the living room.

LIVING ROOM

Sign LIVE, then ROOM. This also applies to FAMILY ROOM: sign FAMILY, then ROOM.

SOFA

This is usually fingerspelled, although the sign in the figure is used sometimes.

COFFEE TABLE

Sign COFFEE, then TABLE.

LAMP/LIGHT

The location you sign LAMP should be in relation to its actual location. For instance, the following figure shows the sign for a light on the ceiling.

CEILING LIGHT

Make the same motions for LIGHT, but at a higher location.

For a halogen lamp with the bulb shining upward, sign it as shown in the following photos.

HALOGEN LAMP

Note how the signer uses the OOO mouth morpheme to show luminance.

NEWSPAPER

Bounce the dominant hand on your other hand twice. This is similar to the sign for PRINT.

MAGAZINE
Repeat the motion.

FIREPLACE
The hands are moved in a circular motion to show the fire's blazes.

These words are fingerspelled:

DVD   TV   VCR

KITCHEN

Deaf people often gather in the kitchen (much like hearing people do); this is another cultural tendency of the Deaf community. While nobody really knows why, a possible reason is because the lighting often is better in the kitchen, which makes for more comfortable communication. Also, the kitchen often is a good gathering spot for people—with food, seating, and good company. The following signs relate to the kitchen.

KITCHEN

Flip the hand a bit; this sign is similar to COOK.

COUNTER

This sign is very similar to FLOOR, but it's signed at countertop level.

CABINET

"Open" the doors; repeat the motion. The B handshape may also be used.

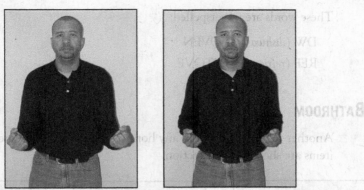

DRAWER

"Open" a drawer; repeat the motion.

TABLE

Bounce your hands on each other twice.

CHAIR

*Bounce the upper two fingers
on the lower two fingers twice.*

MICROWAVE

There are slight variations, but this is the most common version.

These words are fingerspelled:

DW *(dishwasher)* OVEN

REF *(refrigerator)* STOVE

BATHROOM

Another important room in any home is the bathroom. Some common items are shown in this section.

BATHROOM/RESTROOM
Wave the T slightly. This is also the sign for TOILET.

SHOWER
This sign looks like water coming out of a showerhead; repeat the motion.

BATH
Move as if you're washing your chest; repeat the motion.

MIRROR
Shake hand slightly, using the hand as a mirror.

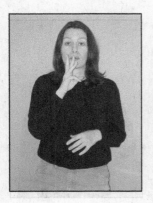

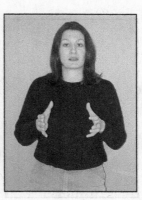

SINK

Sign WATER, then BOWL.

SHAMPOO

Motion as if washing hair. This can also be used for WASH HAIR.

SOAP

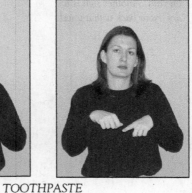

TOOTHBRUSH

Move hand as if brushing teeth; repeat the motion.

TOOTHPASTE

Motion as if squeezing paste on toothbrush; note the use of the 1 handshape to indicate toothbrush.

WASH HANDS

*Rub hands together as if
washing hands.*

BRUSH/COMB

Move as if brushing hair.

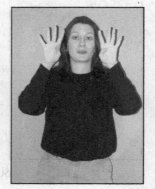

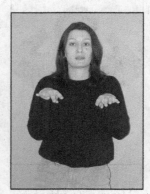

TOWEL (also commonly
fingerspelled)

*Move hand back and forth
on chin. Another sign is to
"dry" your back with a towel.*

CURTAIN

To sign shower curtain, sign SHOWER, then CURTAIN.

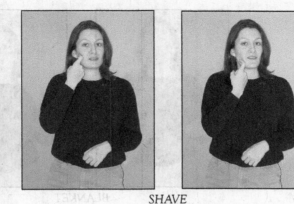

HAIR DRYER

Move the L handshape back and forth as if drying hair.

SHAVE

Be cautious as you sign this; it's very similar to the sign for SEX. A Y handshape may also be used in lieu of the X handshape.

BEDROOM

The bedroom is where we retreat to get our rest and usually keep our clothes. Let's look at some of the things one might find in a bedroom.

BED

PILLOW

Hold a pillow in your hand. Notice puffed cheeks; this shows the fluffiness of the pillow.

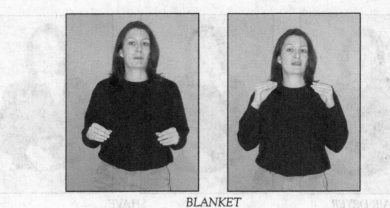

BLANKET

If using a sheet, the handshape would show a less thick sheet by using an F handshape.

DRESSER

This sign is similar to the sign for DRAWER; move your hands down as you "open" multiple drawers.

CLOSET

Bounce the dominant hand on the other hand. There are several variations on this sign; this is the most common version.

CLOTHES

Repeat the motion.

SHOES

Bring the S handshapes together; repeat the motion.

(Neck) TIE

SHIRT   CLOTHES   PANTS

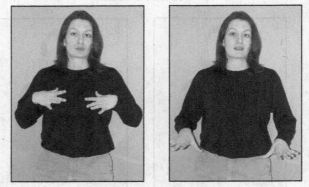

DRESS

This sign is similar to CLOTHES, but it's made with one motion while the sign for CLOTHES has repeated motions. To sign SKIRT, make the same sign starting at the hips.

SHORTS

Show the "cut-off" of pants.

GET-UP (*get up in the morning*)

TIRED

SLEEP

OTHER

We've looked at common rooms within a home. Let's learn the signs for other rooms and items that a home may have.

BASEMENT

Move the hand with the pro-truding thumb in a circular motion while the other palm stays stationary.

WASHER

Both hands twist slightly and quickly to show clothes being washed; this sign may also be used for WASH CLOTHES.

DRYER

This is different from DRY in one way: The sign is repeated in quick, successive motions.

GARAGE

The 3 handshape shows a car going into the garage.

HALL

This sign may also be fingerspelled.

INSIDE

Repeat the motion; a singular motion means IN.

OUTSIDE

*Repeat the motion; this word has several regional variations,
but this is the common version.*

These words are fingerspelled:

AC *(air conditioner)*

ATTIC

HEAT *(can also be signed HOT)*

FAN *(can also be shown by a finger making a big circle repeatedly, like a fan whirring)*

PORCH

REC ROOM *(fingerspell REC then sign ROOM)*

YARD

LOCATION OF THINGS

There are times you'll need to tell someone where something is. What if you're in the kitchen and need something from the bedroom? You can ask someone to get it for you, but you'll need to tell where it is. In ASL, you always sign about things from *your* perspective. For instance, if you say that the door is on the right, it means *your* right—and the other person will understand that it means his left.

Distance can be conveyed by nonmanual signals. For instance, if the plate is within immediate proximity—on the first shelf, for example—the CS mouth morpheme is used.

If the plate is moderately near—on the middle shelf, let's say—the lips are pursed.

However, if the plate is in a far or hard-to-reach shelf, the mouth is opened with a squint of the eyes.

CS *is usually used to show immediate proximity.*

Pursed lips show moderate proximity.

An open mouth and squinted eyes show distance.

These three types of nonmanual signals expressing distance can be applied to many other things—distance of rooms down a hallway, distance of things, and distance in general.

HANDS-ON PRACTICE

Here are two exercises to help you practice what you've learned in this hour:

- Walk through your home and look at different things in each room. Identify the item, where it's located, and if possible, practice with a signer. Ask your fellow signer to retrieve something or move something.

- Look at a furniture catalog and describe the different items and their locations.

HOUR'S UP!

Here's a quiz to help you review some of the facts and ideas presented during this hour. (You can find the correct answers in Appendix A.)

1. What is the signer saying?

  a. The washer and dryer are in the garage.

  b. The washer and dryer are in the basement.

  c. The washer and dryer are in the closet.

  d. The washer and dryer are in the bedroom.

2. True or False: Deaf people have a tendency to gather in the basement.

3. True or False: Nonmanual signals can tell you where something is.

4. What is the signer saying?

a. My aunt is reading the newspaper.

b. My aunt is reading a magazine.

c. My cousin is reading the newspaper.

d. My cousin is reading a magazine.

5. What is the signer saying?

 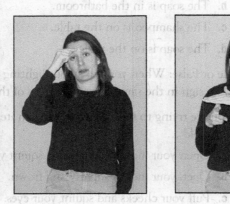 

a. The brown car is outside.

b. The brown car is in the garage.

c. The black car is outside.

d. The black car is in the garage.

6. What does the CS mouth morpheme show?
   a. Depth
   b. Length
   c. Distant proximity
   d. Immediate proximity

7. What is the signer saying?

   a. The shampoo is in the bathroom.
   b. The soap is in the bathroom.
   c. The shampoo is on the table.
   d. The soap is on the table.

8. True or False: When you talk about lighting or lamps, you should always sign in the same place regardless of the type of lighting.

9. If you are trying to tell the location of an item that is very far away, you should …
   a. Open your mouth slightly and squint your eyes.
   b. Open your mouth slightly and frown.
   c. Puff your cheeks and squint your eyes.
   d. Puff your cheeks and frown.

10. What is the signer saying?

a. It's extremely hot outside.

b. It's somewhat hot outside.

c. It's extremely hot inside.

d. It's somewhat hot inside.

VOCABULARY LIST

Here's a summary of the signs you've learned in this hour:

AC (*air conditioner*)	ATTIC
BASEMENT	BATH
BATHROOM/TOILET	BED
BLANKET	BRUSH/COMB
CABINET	CEILING LIGHT
CHAIR	CLOSET
CLOTHES	COFFEE TABLE
COUNTER	CURTAIN
DOOR	DOORBELL
DOWNSTAIRS	DRAWER
DRESS	DRESSER
DRYER	DVD
DW (*dishwasher*)	FAMILY ROOM
FAN	FIREPLACE

FLOOR	GARAGE
GET-UP	HAIR DRYER
HALL	HALOGEN LAMP
HEAT	HOUSE
INSIDE	KITCHEN
LAMP	LIVING ROOM/FAMILY ROOM
MAGAZINE	MICROWAVE
MIRROR	NEWSPAPER
OUTSIDE	OVEN
PANTS	PILLOW
PORCH	REC ROOM (*recreational room*)
REF (*refrigerator*)	ROOF
SHAMPOO	SHAVE
SHIRT	SHOES
SHORTS	SHOWER
SINK	SKIRT
SLEEP	SOAP
SOFA	STAIRS
STOVE	TABLE
TIE (*necktie*)	TIRED
TOOTHBRUSH	TOOTHPASTE
TOWEL	TV
UPSTAIRS	VCR
WALL	WASH HANDS
WASHER	WINDOW
YARD	

RECAP

In this hour, you learned signs for different household items and how to identify their locations. In the next hour, you'll look at identifying and describing
people.

HOUR 17

Talking About People

CHAPTER SUMMARY

LESSON PLAN:

In this hour, you'll learn about ...

- Ways to identify people.
- Descriptions.
- Affirming identifications.

In the hearing community, identifying people is usually done by name reference or by identifying specific parts of their clothing (for example, the woman in the red hat). In ASL, the method is similar, but also described are people's physical appearances, including what some might perceive to be negative aspects of a person's appearance.

This often poses cultural conflicts for people new to the ASL community. Is it polite to say, "See that overweight man? That's Mark."? Not really. But because ASL uses descriptive signs so much, it's accepted in the Deaf community to identify a person by his obvious physical characteristics, such as weight or even beauty marks. Remember how Clerc's name sign was an H on the cheek? That's because he had a scar on his cheek.

If you'd like to identify a person who is present and within sight, there's a specific order for the identification process. First you should identify gender and ethnicity, then height, body type, color of hair and hairstyle, then mention physical appearance (clothing or other noticeable items such as a cane or big earrings), and activity (standing or sitting).

Maybe you're at a hotel and trying to tell your spouse to look at someone you know in the corner. You would say, "See the woman in the corner? The short skinny one, with curly red hair?" Of course, other identifying factors include clothing, distinctive features (for example, the man with the dog or eyeglasses), skin color, and age range (young, old, adult, child).

DESCRIPTIONS

You learned a few adjectives in the previous hours; in this hour you'll look at more people-oriented descriptors.

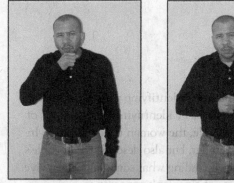

OLD

When using this to describe people, the signer often will bend over slightly, especially to show an old person's posture.

YOUNG

Move hands upward.

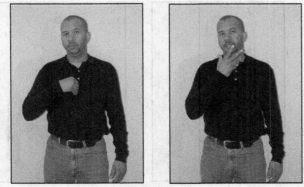

CAUCASIAN

This sign differs from the color WHITE by "throwing" white on the face to indicate Caucasian.

BLACK/AFRICAN AMERICAN

As shown in Hour 16; this can also be used to describe African Americans.

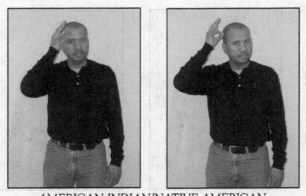

AMERICAN INDIAN/NATIVE AMERICAN

Some American Indians and Alaska Natives use another sign that consists of one hand rubbing the back of the other. At this time, the Intertribal Deaf Council uses the sign in the figure to symbolize various regalia customs such as feather headdresses for many tribes.

ASIAN

There are several variations of this sign; this is the one used by deaf Asians. The old version, still used by many, is an index finger near the eye indicating slanted eyes.

INDIAN

There are several variations of this sign; this is the one most commonly used today.

DARK-SKIN

LIGHT-SKIN is another way of describing skin color.

BLOND

All other hair colors—red, brown, and so on—are signed like the colors shown in Hour 16.

DYE (dyed hair)

Repeat the motion as if dying something.

LONG HAIR

Bring your hands down to the actual length of the hair.

SHORT HAIR

This sign is used for certain styles of short hair, mostly female. Bring the hands up to the length (as opposed to long hair, where you bring the hands down).

SHORT HAIR

This sign is used for hairstyles that are short all around the head, such as a crewcut. Move the hand backward.

BALD

Make a circle on the head using the middle finger, or move the middle finger backward.

STRAIGHT HAIR

CURLY HAIR

Move the hands in circular motions.

BRAIDED

Move the hands down while signing.

PONYTAIL

Bring the hair back into a ponytail. Some signers will do this on their head, instead of in the space in front of the chest.

PIGTAILS

Bring the hands out in "pigtails."

HEADBAND

As if pushing a headband back on the head.

BARRETTE

Indicate where on the head the barrette(s) is. If it is on top of the head, sign it there. If the person has two barrettes, show this by using two hands in the same handshape.

MUSTACHE

Bring the G handshapes down across the top lip.

BEARD

GOATEE

Trace a goatee around the mouth.

GLASSES

Can be used for either sunglasses or eyeglasses; however, a person will often fingerspell SUN if it is sunglasses.

CAP

Move your hand as if putting a baseball cap on.

HAT

Pat your head.

BOWTIE

EARRINGS

Some signers use the F handshape; others use a closed X handshape.

PIERCED NOSE

If the person has an obvious belly ring, sign PIERCE on the navel.

NECKLACE

AFFIRMING AN IDENTIFICATION

Equally important in describing people is being able to locate them or affirm their identity for the person you're talking to. If you are in a crowd and trying to point out someone to your friend or spouse, you need to be able to affirm or negate whether your friend is looking at the right person.

Here's a sample dialogue in English:

Pam: I see Susan!

Willie: Who's Susan?

Pam: She's the tall woman.

Willie: Is that her? (points to different woman)

Pam: No, next to her. The one who's slightly chubby?

Willie: Oh, the one with long hair?

Pam: Yes, that's her! Let's go talk with her.

Willie: Sure.

Let's see how it would look in ASL:

Pam: SUSAN.
Willie: WHO?

Pam: WOMAN TALL.

Willie: THAT?
Pam: NO.

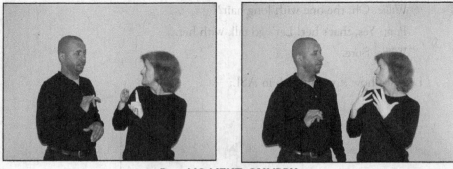

Pam: NO NEXT, CHUBBY.

Willie: LONG HAIR?
Pam: YES!

Pam: GO TALK.
Willie: FINE.

Think about how you'd identify different celebrities. Michael Jordan, for example, is a basketball player. Let's see how the signer describes him.

BLACK

BALD

BASKETBALL

JUMP JUMP/SHOOT

Okay, perhaps the last picture is a bit exaggerated, but you get the idea. First, Jordan's physical appearance is mentioned (one could also add that he's tall), and then his prominent basketball skills are mentioned.

How about Jay Leno? You'd identify him as a man with a prominent chin, comedian, and with streaked gray hair. Or what about Dolly Parton? Bruce Lee? They're all quite easy to describe with their obvious physical features.

HANDS-ON PRACTICE

Try your hands at these exercises:

- A great game to play is the board game Guess?, where different people are shown on a flip-up board. Play this with friends or family, and use physical characteristics to guess who the other person is. Another great game is Old Maid, a card game with different characters.

- Look through magazines and describe the people you see in photographs. Go to the mall and describe people (be subtle so you don't make people feel uneasy or self-conscious) with a fellow signer. Or you can cut out pictures of people from a magazine (or newspaper), and play guessing games with a signer, describing the people until the other guesses the right person.

Hour's Up!

Here's a quiz to help you review some of the facts and ideas presented during this hour. (You can find the correct answers in Appendix A.)

1. True or False: In ASL, people are identified by physical characteristics in addition to names.

2. Which should be used to identify a person first?

   a. Height

   b. Weight

   c. Gender

   d. Skin color

3. True or False: It is not acceptable to identify people by their skin colors in ASL.

4. To describe Bruce Lee, you would sign …

   a. Man, Asian, deceased.

   b. Man, Asian, martial arts expert, deceased.

   c. Man, tall, martial arts expert.

   d. Man, martial arts expert, deceased.

5. Who is the signer describing?

   a. A boy with short curly hair

   b. A short boy with curly hair

   c. A girl with short curly hair

   d. A short girl with curly hair

6. Who is the signer describing?

   a. A short woman with short hair
   b. A tall woman with a hat
   c. A tall man with a hat
   d. A tall man with short hair

7. Who is the signer describing?

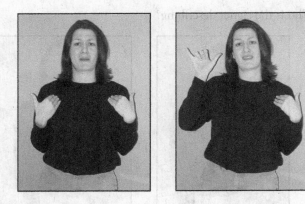

a. A skinny woman with long, blond hair

b. A skinny woman with long, black hair

c. A tall woman with long, black hair

d. A tall woman with long, blond hair

8. What is the signer saying?

a. The tall, skinny man is friendly.

b. The tall, heavy man is crabby.

c. The short, skinny man is friendly.

d. The short, heavy man is crabby.

9. What is the signer saying?

a. The overweight woman is tired.

b. The pregnant woman is tired.

c. The overweight woman is scared.

d. The pregnant woman is scared.

10. Who is the signer describing?

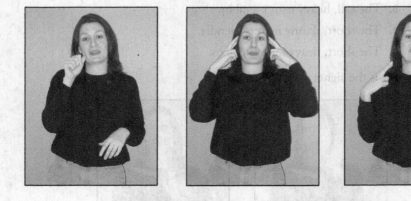

a. The girl with red hair in pigtails

b. The girl with a braided red ponytail and a red bow

c. The girl with red hair in a ponytail

d. The girl with braided pigtails and red bows

QUIZ

VOCABULARY LIST

Here's a summary of the signs you've learned in this hour:

ASIAN	BALD
BARRETTE	BEARD
BLACK/AFRICAN AMERICAN	BLONDE
BOWTIE	BRAIDED HAIR

CAP

CURLY HAIR

DYE

GLASSES

HAT

INDIAN

LONG HAIR

NATIVE AMERICAN/
AMERICAN INDIAN

OLD

PIGTAILS

SHORT HAIR

CAUCASIAN

DARK-SKIN

EARRINGS

GOATEE

HEADBAND

LIGHT-SKIN

MUSTACHE

NECKLACE

PIERCED NOSE

PONYTAIL

STRAIGHT HAIR

YOUNG

RECAP

In this hour, you learned about describing and identifying people. In the next hour, you'll learn the signs for animals.

HOUR 18

Referring to Animals

CHAPTER SUMMARY

LESSON PLAN:

In this hour, you'll learn about ...

- Descriptions.
- Signs for animals.
- Hearing and deaf dogs.

Animals are a part of our lives, whether it be at the zoo, in the house, or on television. Let's learn the signs for critters, small and large, then I'll discuss how to describe them.

ANIMALS

Here are the signs for the most common animals.

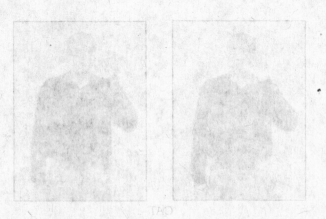

DOG

This way of signing DOG has evolved from the fsidentification of the word. The other way is more common: fingerspelling DOG.

CAT

This can be formed with one or two hands.

ANIMAL

Repeat the motion.

DOG

This way of signing DOG has evolved from the lexicalization of the word. The other way is more common: fingerspelling DOG.

CAT

This can be formed with one or two hands.

FISH

Move the B handshape as if the fish is wiggling.

HORSE

Repeat the motion as if ears are wiggling. The formal version is with both hands on either side of the head, but most use only one hand.

COW

Move the Y handshape much like HORSE; repeat motion. This sign may also be formed with two hands.

PIG

BIRD

Repeat the motion.

SQUIRREL

Repeat the motion of the second step of the sign.

MOUSE

Repeat the motion.

SNAKE

BUG/INSECT

Repeat motion of fingers wiggling.

SPIDER   *TURTLE*

Wiggle fingers.   *Move the thumb in and out as if the turtle is popping its head out and in.*

DEER

Bounce the thumbs on the temple.

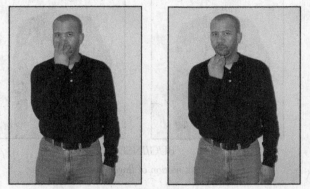

WOLF

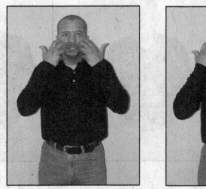 

TIGER

LION

Move hand back over scalp.

ELEPHANT

This illustrates the trunk.

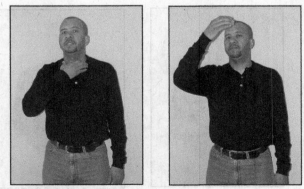

GIRAFFE

GOAT

Make the sign for 12 at the forehead and chin.

SHEEP (LAMB)

"Cut" wool from the sheep; repeat the motion.

MONKEY

Scratch your sides several times.

RABBIT

Another variation is to use the U handshape at the head; this might be confused with HORSE, which has a protruded thumb.

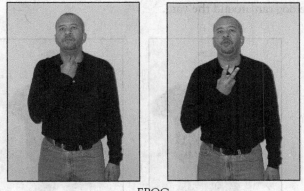

FROG

The sign for 12 is again used here.

DESCRIBING ANIMALS

Describing animals is a little different from describing people, for obvious reasons. Animals have fur or feathers in most cases, and walk differently.

Generally, one should start by naming the animal (if known), then describing the obvious physical traits and characteristics, as seen in the following examples. Nonmanual signals are extremely important when talking about animals; the signer *should* become the animal when signing. The signer's eye gaze should always shift to where the animal is, as if the animal is actually there.

A difference in describing is the skins of animals. They have fur, feathers, or scales. These are described by using classifiers or fingerspelling the words FUR, FEATHER, or SCALE.

Another major difference in describing animals and people is how to describe a walk or motion. When a signer describes people walking, the 1 classifier handshape or the 2 handshape is used. With animals, the 2 or 3 handshapes are the most commonly used handshapes. However, you should always describe the animal exactly how you see it—whether it is on two legs, four legs, or swimming. For example, if an animal gets up on its two rear legs— say a bear or ape walks toward you—you'd change to the 1 handshape to show their two-legged walk.

The dog ran around the yard.

The signer shows how the dog runs around by using his left arm as the yard (with a B handshape), and the dominant hand forms a BENT-V handshape.

The rabbits sat in the garden.

The plurality of RABBIT is shown by the two hands, which indicates two rabbits.

However, for animals like the snake or fish, the absence of legs makes the classifier handshape change to the 1 handshape or B handshape (fish).

The snake slithered toward me, its tongue lashing out.

Notice that in the first picture, the signer's eye gaze looks down at the snake slithering toward him, then in the second picture his eye gaze shifted to the snake looking up and lashing out at the signer. This is yet another important aspect of ASL—the role of eye gaze and "role shifting," where the signer shifts eye gaze to become the other character(s) in the story.

Another way to show the animal's posture is to use the S handshape for posture.

There was a lion with a large mane, poised and waiting to attack.

See how the signer showed his fear when he saw the lion, and showed the lion's posture with the S handshape? Always keep in mind the shape, size, color, and emotion of the situation whenever you're signing a sentence, including those sentences about animals.

HEARING AND DEAF DOGS

Some deaf people have hearing dogs—dogs who are trained to serve deaf people as their "ears." These dogs inform the deaf person when the phone or doorbell rings, and alerts the deaf person to any other sound-related situation, much like visual alerts (flashing lights) do. There are organizations that specialize in hearing dogs, and I've listed a few in Appendix B. They can be any breed, but are placed very carefully after intense training and qualification processes.

Many dogs are also deaf. Unfortunately, some of these dogs are euthanized or abandoned because owners consider them worthless or untrainable. Quite the opposite is true; these dogs are equally intelligent and trainable dogs, and respond extremely well to visual signals.

One of the leading breeds of deaf dogs is the Dalmatian (which is the school mascot for schools such as the Metro Deaf School in St. Paul, Minnesota), but deafness is also commonly found in Great Danes, Pit Bulls, Australian Shepherds, and many other breeds. In fact, deafness is found in pretty much any breed of dog.

A terrific organization devoted to giving these dogs an equal chance to have long and happy lives is DDEAF, the Deaf Dog Education Action Fund (www.deafdogs.org). The organization provides education and funding with the goals of improving and/or saving lives of deaf dogs. The website offers information on dogs available, training information, and a wealth of other resources. Who knows—you might end up adopting a dog through the website!

HANDS-ON PRACTICE

Go to the zoo and observe the animals; you can't get better practice anywhere else. Describe their behaviors, shapes, sizes, colors, skins (fur/feathers), and any other notable characteristics. Try bringing a fluent signer who can show you the finer details of describing animals.

HOUR'S UP!

Here's a quiz to help you review some of the facts and ideas presented during this hour. Some questions have more than one answer. (You can find the correct answers in Appendix A.)

1. What is the signer saying?

    a. The happy dog wagged his tail.

    b. The angry dog wagged his tail.

    c. The happy dog jumped on me.

    d. The angry dog jumped on me.

2. What is the signer describing?

a. A lion

b. A dog

c. A giraffe

d. A cow

3. What are some of the things that differ from describing people when describing animals?

a. Movement

b. Appearance

c. Age

d. Handshapes

4. True or False: The 1 handshape cannot ever be used to describe an animal's movement.

5. What is the signer describing?

a. A horse

b. A cow

c. A rabbit

d. A monkey

6. What is the signer describing?

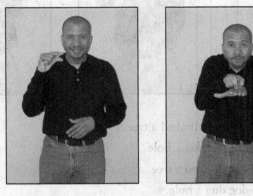

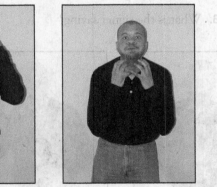

a. A bug

b. A spider

c. A frog

d. A snake

7. What is the signer saying?

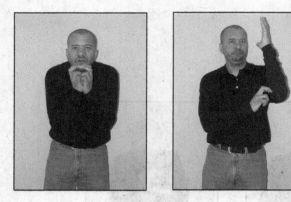

    a. The squirrel climbed a tree.

    b. The squirrel dug a hole.

    c. The cat climbed a tree.

    d. The dog dug a hole.

8. What is the signer saying?

    a. Two dogs jumped on each other and got into a fight.

    b. Two dogs walked into each other.

    c. A dog and a cat got into a fight.

    d. A dog and a cat walked into each other.

9. What is the signer describing?

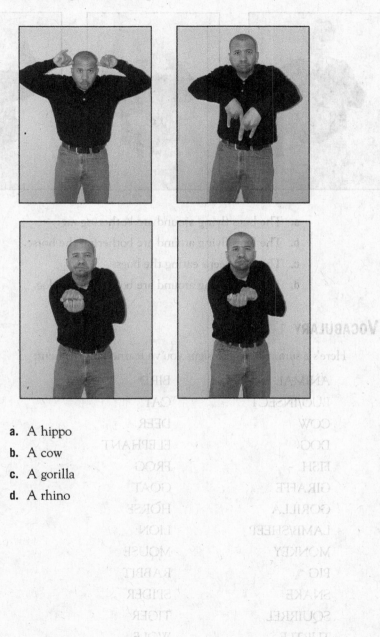

a. A hippo
b. A cow
c. A gorilla
d. A rhino

10. What is the signer saying?

a. The bugs flying around are bothering me.

b. The bugs flying around are bothering the horse.

c. The frog keeps eating the bugs.

d. The bugs flying around are bothering the dog.

VOCABULARY

Here's a summary of the signs you've learned in this hour:

ANIMAL	BIRD
BUG/INSECT	CAT
COW	DEER
DOG	ELEPHANT
FISH	FROG
GIRAFFE	GOAT
GORILLA	HORSE
LAMB/SHEEP	LION
MONKEY	MOUSE
PIG	RABBIT
SNAKE	SPIDER
SQUIRREL	TIGER
TURTLE	WOLF

QUIZ

RECAP

In this hour, you learned about describing and identifying animals. You also learned the difference between describing people and animals. In the next hour, you'll learn the signs for telling time and talking about activities.

HOUR 19

Telling Time

LESSON PLAN:

In this hour, you'll learn about ...

- Telling time.
- Days of the week.
- Months.
- Regularly scheduled activities.

Time controls most of our lives. We use time to meet people, to go to work or school, and for pretty much everything else. Time has an integral role in ASL, especially when used within sentences. In this hour, you'll learn how to communicate the passage of time in ASL.

TELLING TIME

The easiest way to understand how time is used in ASL is to imagine that your body is part of a timeline. Anything in the past is signed near the back of your body or backward; anything in the present is signed near your body; and anything in the future is signed slightly in front of you or forward. The best way to illustrate this is to look at the signs for YESTERDAY, TODAY, and TOMORROW.

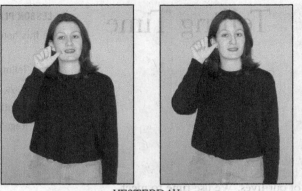

YESTERDAY

Move the thumb backward on the cheek.

TODAY

Bounce the Y handshape twice.

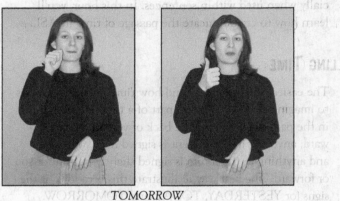

TOMORROW

Move the thumb forward in an arc.

This "timeline" is similar for certain times of the day. Imagine the sun rising and setting—and you'll understand why these words are signed the way they are.

MORNING

AFTERNOON

NIGHT

This sign somewhat resembles a sun rising. Bring the arm up slightly.

Bounce the hand slightly.

DAY

Be sure to use a 1 handshape, not a D handshape. Bring the index finger down to the arm.

However, most signs in ASL are generally not marked by time. So you usually will have to sign the time first, then the sentence. The eyebrows are usually raised when saying time signs.

I went to the dentist yesterday.

YESTERDAY

ME

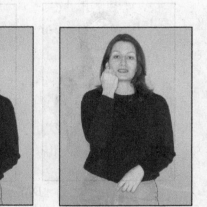

GO

DENTIST

Tomorrow I'll have an appointment in the morning.

TOMORROW

MORNING

APPOINTMENT

HOURS AND MINUTES

Telling time in the form of hours and minutes also is signed in a specific manner.

5:00 A.M.

5 MORNING

Most of the time, you can sign it TIME-6:00, TIME-3:30. However, there is a way to shake the handshape ever so slightly that you do not have to sign time (the best way to see this is to ask a live signer, rather than see a photographed signer). Also, if you've already established the time of the day (that is, saying morning or afternoon), then you don't have to say TIME. Otherwise, you sign time as ordinal numbers: simply sign the numbers facing the other person.

The following signs might be useful for telling time.

HOUR

A clock hand going a full rotation.

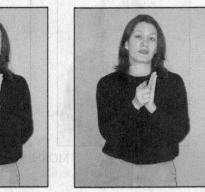

MINUTE

A clock hand moving in minutes.

The word SECOND (as in 30 seconds) is fingerspelled SEC.

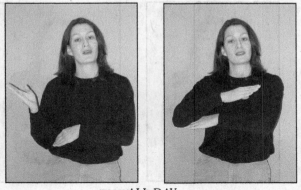

ALL-DAY

The sign for ALL-DAY is similar to DAY, but with a B handshape. Bring the dominant arm over to the other arm in a fluid motion while employing appropriate nonmanual signals (note how the signer tilts her head to show longevity).

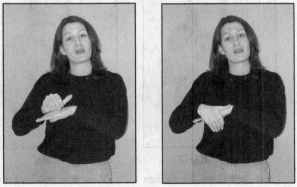

ALL-NIGHT

This sign is generally used to indicate evening hours.

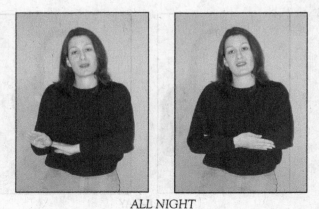

ALL NIGHT

*Move hand/arm in a downward arc. This sign is generally used
to indicate late hours from late evening to early morning.*

MIDNIGHT

*Some people will use the sign
12 instead of a B handshape.*

NOON

*Move your arm back and
forth ever so slightly.*

DAYS, WEEKS, AND MONTHS

Equally important is knowing how to sign days, weeks, and months. First,
let's learn the signs for the days of the week, then you'll learn the weeks and
months. Days are signed in a very small circular motion that is difficult to
show in photographs; the best way to see this motion is to ask a signer to
demonstrate.

SUNDAY

MONDAY

TUESDAY

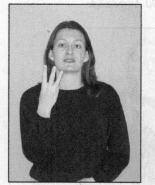

WEDNESDAY

THURSDAY

FRIDAY

Another way to sign
Thursday is to sign T-H.

SATURDAY

WEEK

Imagine you are looking at a calendar. A week is a long bar or
line on a calendar, and this sign indicates that line.

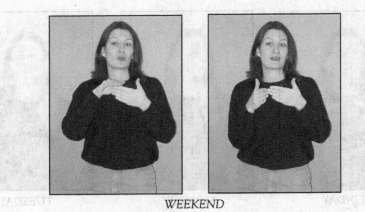

WEEKEND

Bring hand down over nondominant hand at a 90-degree angle.

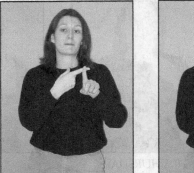

MONTH

Move dominant index finger down while other index finger stays stationary. Again, imagine a calendar. This indicates a whole month.

YEAR

For specific months, you will fingerspell only an abbreviation; for others you will fingerspell the entire month:

JAN	FEB
MARCH	APRIL
MAY	JUNE
JULY	AUG
SEPT	OCT
NOV	DEC

We all do activities either on a regular or irregular basis. ASL has a specific way of telling about these. Here's how you sign these words and other related terms.

DAILY (repeated motion) WEEKLY (repeated motion)
Note how the hands move downward with each week.

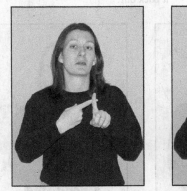

MONTHLY (repeated motion)
Note how the hands move sideways with each month, although some signers move the hands forward.

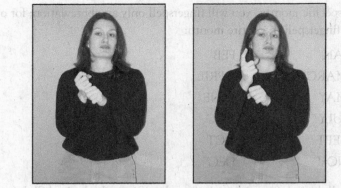

YEARLY *(repeated motion)*

Bring the dominant hand back to the stationary hand. Repeat motion.

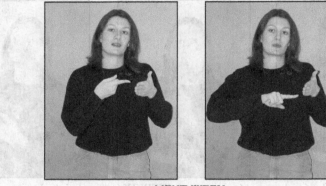

NEXT WEEK

Bring the index finger to the hand then twist it and bring it back out.

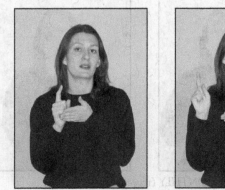

LAST WEEK

NEXT MONTH

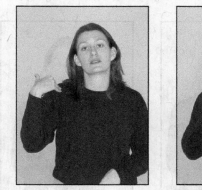

LAST MONTH

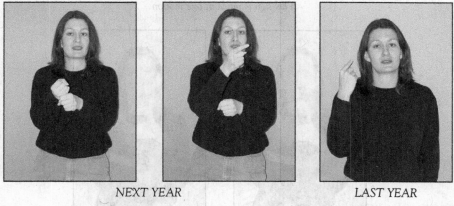

NEXT YEAR

LAST YEAR

Move the index finger up and down while the hand stays stationary.

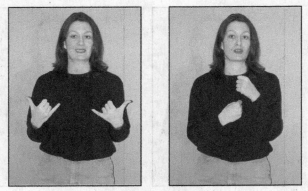

THIS YEAR

Notice how the signer's head slightly moves back while signing THIS.

ONCE

This sign is made in one motion.

OFTEN

Bounce the dominant hand on the other hand twice, but also move the dominant hand up slightly.

SOMETIMES

The eyes are squinted ever so slightly.

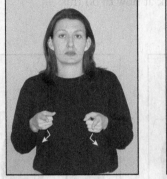

DURING/WHILE

RARELY/SELDOM

The eyes are squinted more intensely than with SOMETIMES, and the sign is made in a slower, fluid, circular motion.

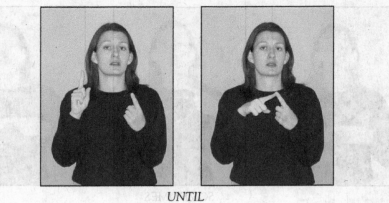

UNTIL

You can also incorporate the numbers 1 through 9 into day, week, and month (1 through 5 for year). Let's look at how to do this:

Two years from now

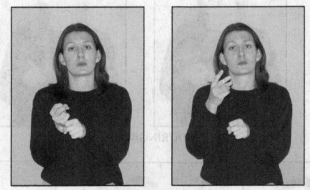

TWO YEARS LATER

Three days (as in *I was there for three days*)

THREE DAYS

Six weeks (as in *I'm in school for six weeks*)

SIX WEEKS

Take a look at some examples to see how time is integrated into sentences.

I go running every morning.

MORNING

The signer moves the sign sideways, which shows that it takes place on a daily/regular basis.

ME   RUN

The meeting will be held next year.

MEETING NEXT YEAR

My doctor's appointment is at 2:00.

2:00 APPOINTMENT DOCTOR

HANDS-ON PRACTICE

Here are some terrific activities you can do to practice what you've learned in this hour:

- Look at a television guide. Look at what scheduled programming is on for this week, and find the regularly scheduled programs; fingerspell the show titles, practice the times, and fingerspell the actors' names.

- Look at your own date book or calendar and practice signing what activities you had in the last month or will have in the next month.

Hour's Up!

Here's a quiz to help you review some of the facts and ideas presented during this hour. List on the calendar what each signer says. Today is Thursday the 10th. (You can find the correct answers in Appendix A.)

SUNDAY	MONDAY	TUESDAY	WEDNESDAY	THURSDAY	FRIDAY	SATURDAY
		1	2	3	4	5
6	7	8	9	10	11	12
13	14	15	16	17	18	19
20	21	22	23	24	25	26
27	28	29	30			

1.

2.

3.

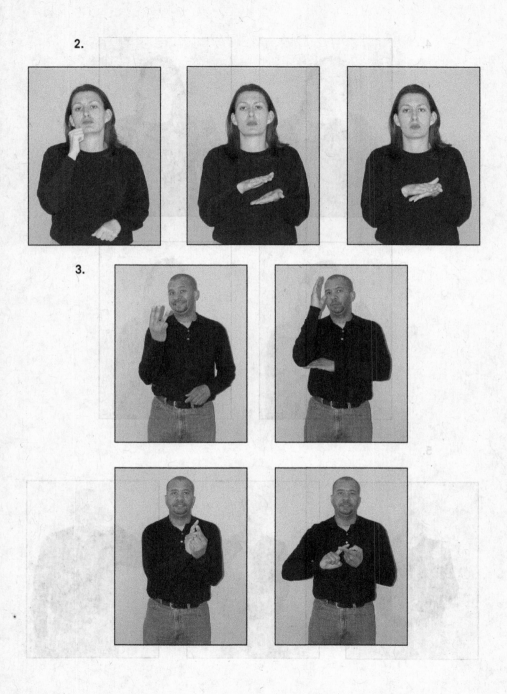

4.

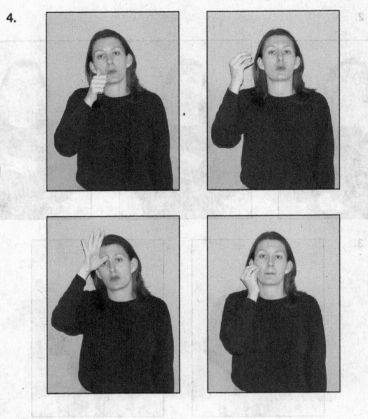

5.

6.

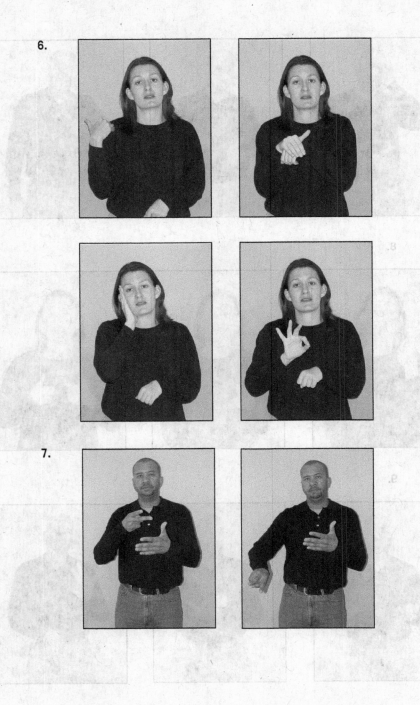

7.

8.

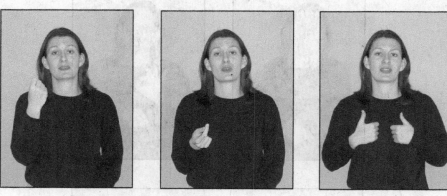

9.

10.

QUIZ

VOCABULARY LIST

Here's a summary of the signs you've learned in this hour.

AFTERNOON	ALL DAY
ALL NIGHT	DAILY
DAY	DURING/WHILE
FRIDAY	HOUR
JAN through DEC	LAST MONTH
LAST WEEK	LAST YEAR
MIDNIGHT	MINUTE
MONDAY	MONTH
MONTHLY	MORNING
NEXT MONTH	NEXT WEEK

NEXT YEAR	NIGHT
NOON	OFTEN
RARELY	SATURDAY
SOMETIMES	SUNDAY
THIS YEAR	THURSDAY
TODAY	TOMORROW
TUESDAY	UNTIL
WEDNESDAY	WEEK
WEEKEND	WEEKLY
YEAR	YEARLY
YESTERDAY	

RECAP

In this hour, you learned how ASL incorporates time into statements. You also learned to tell time and to identify different parts of the day, week, month, and year. In the next hour, we'll go to work at the office.

PART V

Talking About
Your Life

PART V

Talking About
Your Life

HOUR 20

Working in the Office

LESSON PLAN:

In this hour, you'll learn about ...

- Employment and deaf people.
- Occupations.
- Office supplies and furniture.

Today, deaf people work in every job field imaginable. There are deaf engineers, doctors, veterinarians, lawyers, administrators, mechanics, writers, interior designers, postal workers, artists, and many more. This is remarkable, given the misconceptions deaf people often have to overcome.

In the past, deaf people often were offered inadequate opportunities in the working world. Dealing with misconceptions, stereotypes, and mistaken assumptions about intelligence and capabilities was and often is a fact of life for the majority of deaf people.

Deaf people also might be turned down for jobs because of audio-related duties: phone duties, communication with other people, and so on. The Americans with Disabilities Act and other laws were designed to protect deaf people from discrimination at work or in the hiring process, but unfortunately, this doesn't always happen. Some employers are wary of the costs associated with accommodating a deaf employee, but the final total usually is less than $1,000. Many employers are also unaware of how capable deaf people are.

Deaf people have proven time after time that they are equal to, if not better than, their hearing co-workers. Online communication has also paved the way for easier communication. Deaf people can now e-mail their bosses or converse with workers via pagers or instant messaging, and be given access to information that they otherwise would not have had 10 years ago. Relay services have also helped deaf people place calls at work or online, and video relay services or video interpreting services have helped ease the burden of trying to find a qualified interpreter. Although the job market is a long way from equal for deaf people, it's at a far better point than it was a few years ago.

OCCUPATIONS

ASL users often, rather than saying, "He's an accountant," will say, "HE WORK ACCOUNTING." So what I've elected to do here is show you the sign for the occupation, rather than the position. For instance, I'll show you the sign for *Accounting* rather than *Accountant*, but the caption will list the position. However, some signs, such as LAWYER, might be signed as LAW + PERSON, depending on the individual style of the signer.

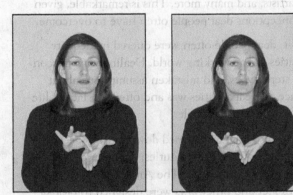

ACCOUNTANT
Repeat motion. This is also the sign for COUNT.

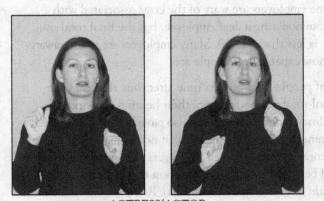

ACTRESS/ACTOR
Some signers use the S handshape instead of the A handshape.

ARTIST

BOSS

Bounce the open C hand-shape on your shoulder.

CARPENTER

CASHIER

"Slide" the S handshape across the open palm. Repeat motion.

Move hand as if typing on a register

CONSTRUCTION (WORKER)

This sign is similar to BUILD.

COOK

DEALER/SELLER (one who sells something; for example, a car dealer)

DENTIST

Bounce the sign on the side of the mouth; this is one of several variations.

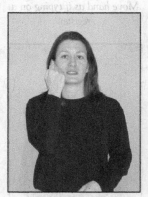

DENTIST

Bounce the sign on the side of the mouth; this is one of several variations.

ENGINEER

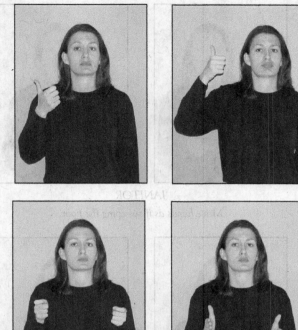

EXECUTIVE DIRECTOR

The sign used for EXECUTIVE is normally used to show superiority and authority. This sign can also be used for BIG when saying "my big boss" or HIGHER-UP. Note the facial expression.

FARMER

Bring the hand from one side of the face to the other.

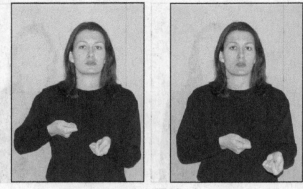

JANITOR

Move hands as if sweeping the floor.

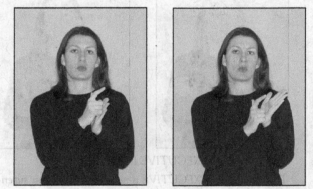

LAWYER

Move L handshape down on palm of other hand.

LIBRARIAN

*Move the L handshape in
a circular motion.*

MANAGER

Move hands in opposing directions.

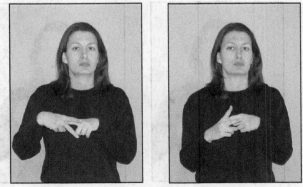

MECHANIC/PLUMBER

To distinguish between the two words, insert CAR or
BATHROOM/WATER before signing the word.

PILOT (*Airport worker*)   **PRESIDENT**

Move hand back and forth
slightly to show "flying."

PSYCHOLOGIST

Bounce the dominant hand slightly.

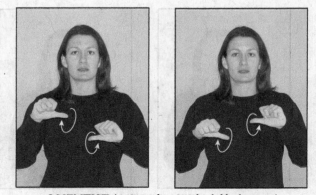

SCIENTIST (or one who is in the field of science)

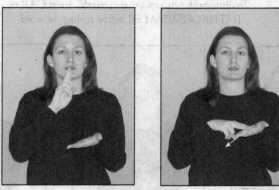

SECRETARY

Other variations include substituting the K handshape with a U handshape or closed X handshape, but in the same motion.

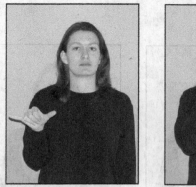

STAY HOME

Move the Y handshape down slightly, then sign HOME. This sign is used to sign stay-at-home mom or dad or work from home. Add the sign for MOM, DAD, and so on.

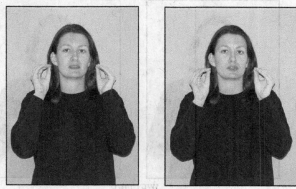

TEACHER

Move both hands out from the head slightly; repeat the motion.

VICE PRESIDENT

Also commonly fingerspelled as V-P.

WAITER/WAITRESS

Move both hands in opposing directions. Repeat the motion.

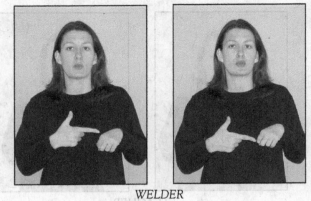

WELDER
Repeat the motion.

FURNITURE AND SUPPLIES

An office needs furniture and supplies. So let's learn the signs for these.

BUSINESS CARD

BOOK
This sign can be used for binder, folder, and so on.

CLOCK

COMPUTER

Move both hands in small circles. This is one of several versions.

COMPUTER

This is one of several versions.

COPIER

Sign COPY and then MACHINE.

DESK

*This sign is similar to TABLE;
bounce the hands on arms.*

ENVELOPE

Lick the envelope then show the shape.

FAX

Indicate a piece of paper coming through the fax machine. Although this seems to be somewhat standardized, a majority of signers still fingerspell the word.

FILE

Put paper in a "file folder."

LETTER

MACHINE

Note the signer's nonmanual signals; this shows the machine's vibrations or noises.

OFFICE

This sign is similar to ROOM, with an O handshape. It's also commonly fingerspelled.

PAGER

A new sign that has developed within the past five years, thanks to the advent of two-way pagers.

PAPER

PAPER CLIP   PEN/PENCIL

SCANNER

Move the X handshape back and forth as if scanning.

SCISSORS

STAMP

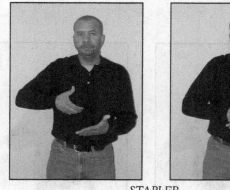

STAPLER

These words are fingerspelled:

EMAIL (There are several signs that have emerged, but none have become standardized nor official yet.)

TTY

WORK DUTIES AND ACTIVITIES

You've learned different signs for occupations and careers, in addition to office furniture and items. Now you'll learn the signs for different activities and duties commonly performed at work.

TYPE   WRITE

Sign as if typing.   *Repeat the motion.*

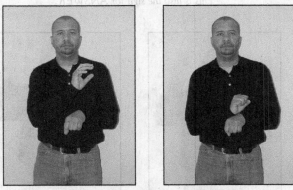

APPOINTMENT (*also* RESERVE)

CONTACT

Repeated motions of 3 or 4 times mean keeping in touch constantly.

REPORT

This is also the sign for ANSWER.

INFORM

FILL OUT (forms)

READ

RUN (a meeting)
Repeat the motion.

MEETING

Bring the fingers into a closed O handshape; repeat the motion.

PICK UP (*a package; something from the floor*)

DELIVER

This is similar to BRING.

BREAK (*take a break*)

HANDS-ON PRACTICE

Look in the employment ad section of your newspaper. Practice signing the different occupations and duties listed, along with the names and phone numbers. Or go to an office supply store, and practice signing the items you see there (you could also visit office supplies websites).

HOUR'S UP!

Here's a quiz to help you review some of the facts and ideas presented during this hour. (You can find the correct answers in Appendix A.)

1. What does the signer do for a living?

   a. Work with money

   b. Work with people

   c. Work with computers

   d. Work with animals

2. What position does the signer hold?

   a. President

   b. Executive Director

   c. Big boss

   d. Supervisor

3. What does the signer do for a living?

a. Construction
b. Teach science
c. Teach reading
d. Computer work

4. What does the signer do at work?

a. Sell cars
b. Sell computers
c. Sell clothes
d. Sell copiers

5. What position does the signer hold?

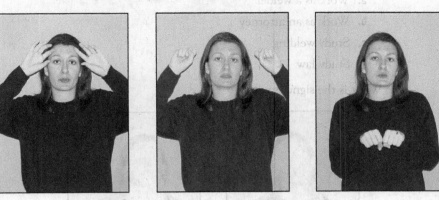

a. President of a car company

b. Vice president of a car company

c. President of a shoe company

d. Vice president of a shoe company

6. What does the signer do?

a. Work as a welder

b. Work as an attorney

c. Study welding

d. Study law

7. What is the signer saying?

a. I'm going to the break room and get food.

b. I'm taking a break and eating.

c. I'm going to eat in the break room.

d. I'm going to get something to eat then take a break.

8. What does the signer need to do?

a. Buy pens

b. Buy paper

c. Pick up pens

d. Pick up paper

9. What did the signer do?

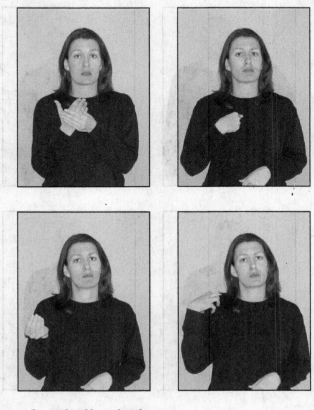

a. Gave the file to her boss

b. Filed a report for the boss

c. Gave a report to the secretary to file

d. Filed a report for the secretary

10. What is the signer saying?

a. My secretary just paged to let me know there's a meeting today.

b. My secretary just faxed to let me know there's a meeting today.

c. My boss just paged to let me know there's a meeting today.

d. My boss just faxed to let me know there's a meeting today.

VOCABULARY LIST

Here's a summary of the signs you've learned in this hour:

ACCOUNTANT	ACTRESS/ACTOR
APPOINTMENT	ARTIST
BOOK	BOSS
BREAK	BUSINESS CARD
CARPENTER	CASHIER

QUIZ

CLOCK
CONSTRUCTION (WORKER)
COOK
DEALER/SELLER
DENTIST
ENGINEER
EXECUTIVE DIRECTOR
FAX
FILL OUT
JANITOR
LETTER
MACHINE
MECHANIC
OFFICE
PAPER
PEN/PENCIL
PILOT
PRESIDENT
READ
SCANNER
SCISSORS
STAMP
STAY HOME
TYPE
WAITER/WAITRESS
WRITE

COMPUTER
CONTACT
COPIER
DELIVER
DESK
ENVELOPE
FARMER
FILE
INFORM
LAWYER
LIBRARIAN
MANAGER
MEETING
PAGER
PAPER CLIP
PICK UP
PLUMBER
PSYCHOLOGIST
RUN
SCIENTIST
SECRETARY
STAPLER
TEACHER
VICE PRESIDENT
WELDER

RECAP

In this hour, you learned about deaf people's employment opportunities. You also learned the signs for different occupations, along with various office supplies and duties. In the next hour, we'll go out to eat.

CLOCK	COMPUTER
	CONSTRUCTION (WORKER) CONTACT
COOK	COPIER
DEALER/SELLER	DELIVER
DENTIST	DESK
ENGINEER	ENVELOPE
EXECUTIVE DIRECTOR	FARMER
FAX	FILE
FILL OUT	INFORM
JANITOR	LAWYER
LETTER	LIBRARIAN
MACHINE	MANAGER
MECHANIC	MEETING
OFFICE	PAGER
PAPER	PAPER CLIP
PEN/PENCIL	PICK UP
PILOT	PLUMBER
PRESIDENT	PSYCHOLOGIST
READ	RUN
SCANNER	SCIENTIST
SCISSORS	SECRETARY
STAMP	STAPLER
STAY/HOME	TEACHER
TYPE	VICE PRESIDENT
WAITER/WAITRESS	WELDER
WRITE	

RECAP

In this hour, you learned about deaf people's employment opportunities. You also learned the signs for different occupations, along with various office supplies and duties. In the next hour, we'll go on to eat...

HOUR 21

Eating Out

CHAPTER SUMMARY

LESSON PLAN:

In this hour, you'll learn about ...

- The restaurant experience.
- Food signs.
- Condiment signs.
- Common requests.

Eating out at restaurants is something that everyone does at one time or another. Deaf people love eating out as much as hearing people, especially because it's a great opportunity for them to gather. It can be an especially interesting experience to eat at a restaurant as a deaf person, especially if the waiter or waitress doesn't quite know how to communicate with deaf people.

In many cases, the deaf person will simply point to items on the menu, and write down any additional information not found on the menu. Gestures are also used. Yet others will speak for themselves.

THE RESTAURANT EXPERIENCE

An interesting scene often happens if a group of deaf people goes out to eat and one of the group members can speak. If that person orders first, the waiter usually will assume that the person will be speaking for the entire group, and rely upon that person instead of asking each individual. If you are hearing, this probably will happen to you. This isn't only burdensome on you, but it also gives the waiter the impression that nonspeaking deaf people cannot order for themselves. A solution is to order last, so that the each member of the group can communicate for him or herself.

Other barriers deaf people often face in eating out include being placed in locations where they're not visible to other customers (in case their signing "scares off" potential hearing customers), ignorance on the part of the restaurant personnel, and lousy service (which is an experience shared by hearing people, as well). Some waiters will simply not check in often with deaf people after taking their orders, because they feel communication is too cumbersome. There have even been situations where deaf people are refused paper and pen.

The best solution to these situations is usually patience and awareness training, especially on the part of restaurant workers. Today, more and more waiters and waitresses actually know sign language, thanks to improved awareness. The bottom line: The dining experience is usually as pleasant for deaf people as it is for hearing people.

RESTAURANT AND FOOD SIGNS

Let's start with a general overview of the most common signs you'll use when eating out.

RESTAURANT

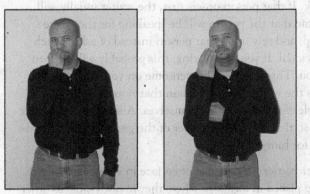

BREAKFAST (EAT + MORNING)

*It is important to note that many signers sign this word with a
B on the chin.*

LUNCH (EAT + NOON)

Many signers sign this with a L on the chin.

DINNER (EAT + NIGHT)

Many signers sign this with a D or S (for SUPPER) at the chin.

HUNGRY

Move the hand down the chest.

THIRSTY

Move the finger down the throat.

COOK   PLATE

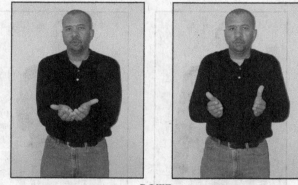

BOWL

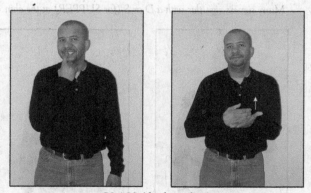

GLASS *(drinking glass)*

*Sign GLASS (first picture) then bring the C handshape up to
indicate it's a drinking glass.*

CUP

Bounce the C handshape on the other hand.

FORK

Bounce the "fork" against your other hand. Some people use the W handshape instead of the V handshape.

SPOON

KNIFE

Move only the dominant hand; if both hands are moved, that becomes the sign for EGG.

NAPKIN

Move the hand back and
forth over the chin/mouth.

SODA

COFFEE

Move the top hand in a circular motion, as if grinding
coffee beans.

TEA

Move the fingers in a circle
inside of the other hand.

MILK

Move hands as if milking a cow.

BEER

WINE

This is a quick, repeated motion; a singular motion changes the sign to BROWN.

Move the hand in a small circular motion on the cheek.

EGG

Crack open an egg.

BACON

TOAST

SOUP

This sign is similar to SPOON, but the nondominant hand is a curved palm.

SALAD

Toss a salad.

FRUIT

Move the F slightly back and forth without leaving the cheek.

VEGETABLE

This sign is similar to FRUIT; it's commonly fingerspelled VEG.

BREAD

SANDWICH

Bring the hand to the mouth repeatedly; this is the first of two variations.

SANDWICH

Bounce the dominant hand repeatedly; this is the second of the two variations.

CHICKEN

HAMBURGER

This sign is similar to BIRD.

HOT DOG

FRENCH FRIES

POTATO

*Bounce the BENT-V hand-
shape on top of the other hand.*

MEAT

*This sign can also be used
for STEAK.*

SPAGHETTI

*Repeat motion. Some people bring the hands together (as shown
here); others bring the hands apart in the opposite direction.*

STRICTLY DEFINED

PIZZA

This is actually only part of the word "pizza." The signer is showing how the double Z is fingerspelled: with both the first and middle fingers. Normally, it would be fingerspelled as P-I-ZZ-A. Fluent fingerspellers will often sign "ZZ-A".

CHEESE

DESSERT

This sign is similar to DATE.

CONDIMENTS AND EXTRAS

And let's not forget condiments or extras.

SALT

Move either finger up and down in repeated motions.

PEPPER

This sign is similar to FRENCH FRIES, but with different nonmanual signals.

SUGAR

This is also the sign for SWEET.

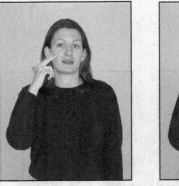

KETCHUP

Ketchup is a word with many regional variations; this is one.

KETCHUP

"Shake" a ketchup bottle on the dish.

DRESSING *(pour dressing over salad)*

SMALL (MEDIUM, LARGE)

To say SMALL, MEDIUM, or LARGE, simply fingerspell the first letter (S, M, or L).

MORE

PLEASE *THANK YOU*

FULL

The following words are fingerspelled:

APPETIZER   MAYO

Hands-On Practice

To practice your newly learned signing skills, check out these exercises:

- Read newspaper or magazine reviews of restaurants, and practice fingerspelling the restaurant name, location, main dishes, and any other information contained in the review.

- Get menus from your local restaurants. Sign the different dishes, describe them, and sign the costs.

HOUR'S UP!

Here's a quiz to help you review some of the facts and ideas presented during this hour. (You can find the correct answers in Appendix A.)

1. What did the signer order?

   a. Chicken sandwich
   b. Chicken salad
   c. Chicken and potatoes
   d. Chicken and fries

2. What drink does the signer want?

   a. Milk
   b. Tea
   c. Coffee
   d. Soda

3. What is the signer saying?

   a. I'm so hungry; I want steak.

   b. I'm so thirsty; I want water.

   c. I'm so hungry; I want pizza.

   d. I'm so thirsty; I want milk.

4. Which item on the menu did the signer order?

   a. A hot dog with ketchup

   b. A chicken sandwich with cheese

   c. A steak with A-1

   d. A cheeseburger

5. What did the signer have for lunch?

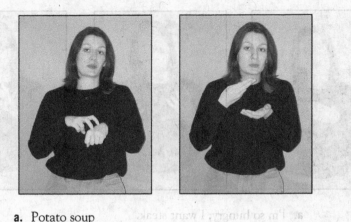

    a. Potato soup

    b. French onion soup

    c. Broccoli and cheese soup

    d. Chicken noodle soup

6. Which special is the signer having?

    a. Soup with bread

    b. Chicken with fries

    c. Fish fry with bread

    d. Fish with fries

7. What sandwich does the signer want?

    a. A meatball sandwich

    b. A fish sandwich

    c. A chicken sandwich

    d. A cheese steak sandwich

8. What is the signer drinking with her dinner?

    a. Wine

    b. Beer

    c. Water

    d. Milk

9. What would the signer like?

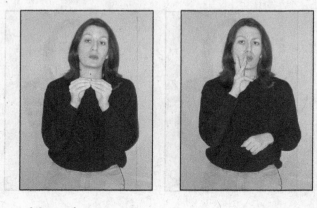

   a. More salt
   b. More pepper
   c. More wine
   d. More water

10. How much did the signer's dinner cost?

   a. $8.48
   b. $8.57
   c. $9.48
   d. $9.57

QUIZ

VOCABULARY LIST

Here's a summary of the signs you've learned in this hour.

BACON	BEER
BOWL	BREAD
BREAKFAST	CHEESE
CHICKEN	COFFEE
COOK	CUP
DESSERT	DINNER
DRESSING	EGG
FORK	FRENCH FRIES
FRUIT	FULL
GLASS	HAMBURGER
HOT DOG	HUNGRY
KETCHUP	KNIFE
LUNCH	MEAT
MILK	MORE
NAPKIN	PEPPER
PIZZA	PLATE
PLEASE	POTATO
RESTAURANT	SALAD
SALT	SANDWICH
SMALL (MEDIUM, LARGE)	SODA
SOUP	SPAGHETTI
SPOON	SUGAR
TEA	THANK YOU
THIRSTY	TOAST
VEGETABLE	WINE

RECAP

In this hour, you learned about how eating out for deaf people is sometimes a unique experience. You learned various signs for use at a restaurant. In the next hour, you'll learn the signs associated with being ill.

HOUR 22

Being Sick

Being sick is never any fun. Most of us have had the flu at one time or another, the chicken pox, or even the common cold. We discussed the problems of interpreters and communication accessibility in Hour 13. In this hour, you'll learn how lack of communication access can impact deaf people, and more.

COMMUNICATING DISTRESS

Unfortunately, the problems facing deaf people in terms of communication accessibility are also often true for doctors' offices and extended hospital stays. Although many hospitals provide interpreters upon request, many deaf people do not realize they are entitled to this by law. There has been case after case in which hospitals or doctors denied deaf people access to interpreters or reasonable accommodations (such as captioned television for extended hospital stays). Others have also been refused interpreters for births, emergency situations, and doctor visits. This is dangerous, especially if the deaf person does not receive appropriate communication about medication dosages or medical options.

Doctors are facing outrageous malpractice insurance costs, and health insurance costs are skyrocketing. Many doctors are now refusing to serve deaf people at all, rather than footing the extra $100 or so for a two-hour interpreter request. The law is vague on this, and it is cause for much controversy today.

Another factor in the struggle for interpreter services for hospital or doctor visits—especially emergencies—is that interpreters often are not available for last-minute requests. Some interpreter agencies do have 24-hour, on-call interpreter services, but demand is often higher than supply.

Some hospitals are now turning to video remote interpreting services (VRI, sometimes known as VIS). During VRI, interpreters are on call; doctors can dial up the VRI agency to request interpreter service through video connections. This is a new trend that is slowly catching on at hospitals and doctors' offices across the country. Although VRI can be costly, it's a lot less costly than losing a person's life.

With advocacy and awareness training taking place to ensure that qualified, certified interpreters are available upon demand, and hospitals/doctors realizing that communication is essential to maintaining health, deaf people can look forward to improved experiences in the future.

HEALTH-RELATED SIGNS

People often talk about common ailments or major health situations with friends or family. The following signs communicate some of the more common ailments.

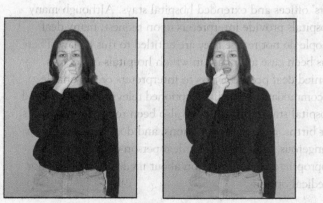

COLD

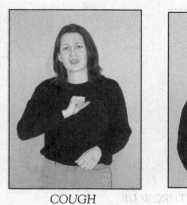

COUGH

Pound your chest slightly.

THROAT HURT (*sore throat*)

HEADACHE

EAR INFECTION

Shake the I handshape slightly.

CHILLS

This sign is similar to the sign for COLD (cold water), but with more tense shivering.

SWEAT

TEMPERATURE

Move the index finger up and down on the other finger.

THROW UP

Move hands in small forward arc.

NAUSEA

Move the hand in a circular motion on the stomach.

DIZZY

Move both hands in small circular motions.

SICK

NOT FEEL GOOD

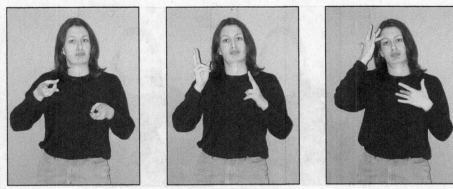

SUDDENLY SICK

The first two steps of this sign have no direct English translation; however, the whole phrase means suddenly becoming sick.

WEAK

BLEED

Repeat the motion.

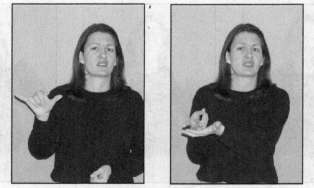

STAY BED (2 handshape)

This sign is most often used in sentences like, "He was in bed the whole week he was sick."

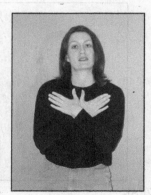 

REST   MEDICINE

Notice that this sign is made in the same location as DOCTOR and NURSE.

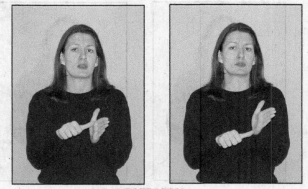

OPERATION

Move thumb down in straight direction. This sign may be made on other parts of the body to indicate surgery on the leg, arm, stomach, heart, and so on. See the following sign for an example.

STOMACH
OPERATION

Note how the same sign is made at a different location.

DISEASE

DISEASE is similar to SICK, but made with quick, repeated motions.

HEART ATTACK

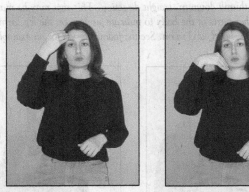

STROKE

Bring the hand down from the head.

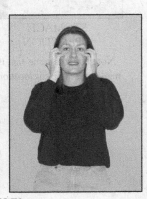

MEASLES

This shows "dots" all over the face.

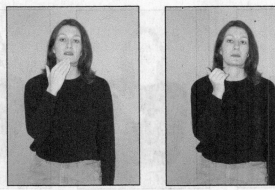

DIABETES

This is also the sign for SWEET/SUGAR.

TOOTH PULL OUT

ALLERGY

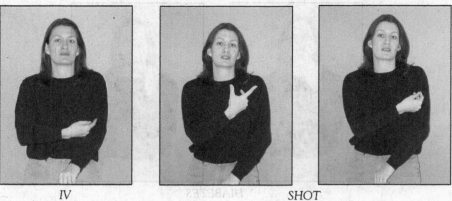

IV

SHOT

Make the sign, then finger-spell I–V.

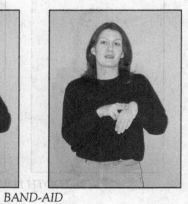

BAND-AID

Move two fingers back across other hand, as if putting on a Band-Aid.

BETTER

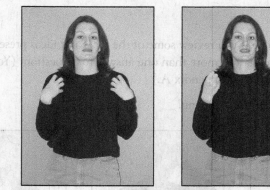

GET WELL/RECUPERATE

PHARMACY (MEDICINE STORE)

The following words are fingerspelled:

CANCER

CHICKEN POX (sign CHICKEN, then fingerspell POX)

FEVER (can be signed as TEMPERATURE)

FLU

NUMB (can be signed as FEEL-NONE)

HANDS-ON PRACTICE

To practice the new words you've just learned, go to the pharmacy and look at different over-the-counter medications or supplies (gauze, bandages, and so on) and practice describing the illnesses or conditions that these items are used for.

HOUR'S UP!

Here's a quiz to help you review some of the facts and ideas presented during this hour. There may be more than one answer to a question. (You can find the correct answers in Appendix A.)

1. What is the signer saying?

   a. I'm sick with a sore throat.

   b. I'm sick and feeling weak.

   c. I'm sick with a cold.

   d. I'm sick and feeling cold.

2. True or False: Some hospitals are now turning to video remote interpreting to meet the needs of deaf patients.

3. What is wrong with the signer?

    a. He had a sore throat and threw up.

    b. He had nausea and threw up.

    c. He had a headache and threw up.

    d. He had a cold and threw up.

4. What is the signer saying?

    a. My temperature is 97 degrees.

    b. My temperature is 98 degrees.

    c. My temperature is 99 degrees.

    d. My temperature is 100 degrees.

5. Why should an interpreter be certified and qualified to do medical interpreting?

    a. Miscommunication could result in serious injury or death.

    b. The doctor needs to be able to communicate clearly with the deaf patient.

    c. Essential information could be lost if the interpreter isn't qualified or certified.

    d. The patient deserves full communication access.

6. What is the signer saying?

    a. He had surgery, so he stayed at the hospital.

    b. He had a heart attack, so he stayed at the hospital.

    c. He had a sore throat, so he stayed home.

    d. He had a cold, so he stayed home.

7. What is the signer saying?

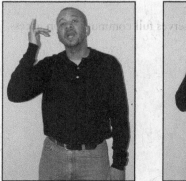 

a. I have an appointment at the doctor tomorrow for a cold.

b. I have an appointment at the doctor tomorrow for a sore throat.

c. I have an appointment at the hospital today for a surgery.

d. I have an appointment at the hospital to get medication.

8. What is the signer saying?

a. Today the dentist pulled my tooth.

b. Today the doctor gave me a shot.

c. Yesterday the dentist pulled my tooth.

d. Yesterday the doctor gave me a shot.

9. What did the doctor say?

    a. The medicine should be taken with milk.

    b. The medicine should be taken with water.

    c. The medicine should be taken with food.

    d. The medicine should be taken before bed.

10. What is the signer saying?

    a. Dad went to get his tooth pulled out.

    b. Mom went to get her tooth pulled out.

    c. Dad went to get his shots.

    d. Mom went to get her shots.

QUIZ

VOCABULARY LIST

Here's a summary of the signs you've learned in this hour.

ALLERGY	BANDAID
BETTER	BLEED
CHILLS	COLD
COUGH	DIABETES
DISEASE	DIZZY
EAR INFECTION	GET WELL/RECUPERATE
HEADACHE	HEART ATTACK
IV	MEASLES
MEDICINE	NAUSEA
NOT FEEL GOOD	OPERATION
PHARMACY	REST
SHOT	SICK
STAY BED	STROKE
SUDDENLY SICK	SWEAT
TEMPERATURE	THROAT HURT
THROW UP	TOOTH PULL OUT
WEAK	

RECAP

In this hour, you learned about deaf people's experiences with hospitals and doctors and the importance of communication access. You also learned the signs for common ailments. In the next hour, we'll play some sports.

HOUR 23

Sports and Recreation

LESSON PLAN:

In this hour, you'll learn about ...

- Deaf people and sports.
- Sports signs.
- Actions and plays.

Sports and recreation are major sources of social opportunities and gatherings for deaf people. Many deaf people are outstanding athletes (although some are klutzes, too). There have been quite a few deaf athletes at the professional level: Curtis Pride (baseball), Luther Taylor (baseball), Richard Sipek (baseball), Kenny Walker (football), and Ronda Jo Miller (basketball); the list goes on and on. Terence Parkin of South Africa made history when he earned a silver medal at the 2000 Olympics. In fact, the involvement of deaf people in professional sports goes back so many years that it'd fill up an entire book.

FYI Deaf people have made great contributions to sports. The football huddle is said to have been invented at Gallaudet College (now University), to prevent opposing teams from reading the deaf quarterback's signs.

William "Dummy" Hoy, who played professional baseball from 1886 to 1903, is credited with inventing the signals used by umpires to indicate strikes and outs because he couldn't hear the umpire.

Sporting events are thriving as popular gathering spots for deaf people. There are national tournaments, local and regional events, and even international competitions. Deaf people participate in the Deaflympics (formerly the World Games of the Deaf), which is held in the winter and the summer, just like the Olympics. There are deaf referees and umpires; Marsha Wetzel became the first deaf female referee to work at the NCAA Division I level in 2003.

The United States of America Deaf Sports Federation is a great resource about sports and deaf people. Check out its website at www.usadsf.org.

SPORTS SIGNS

Many of these signs also have regional variations or school variations (for instance, the Illinois School for the Deaf signs FOOTBALL as if a person is holding the football to his shoulder; Minnesotans sign SNOWMOBILING with a 3 handshape at the shoulder; and so on). However, I've listed the common signs here.

BASEBALL
Motion as if swinging a bat slightly; repeat the motion.

BASKETBALL
Motion as if shooting a ball; repeat the motion.

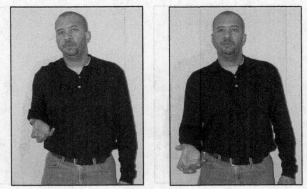

BOWLING

Move hand forward as if throwing a bowling ball.

CAMPING

This sign indicates a tent.

FOOTBALL

Repeat the motion.

GOLF

Swing a club.

HIKING

This is also the sign for WALK; it is often fingerspelled.

HOCKEY

Move the X handshape as if pushing a puck; repeat the motion.

RUNNING

This sign is also used for JOGGING; repeat the motion.

SKIING

Repeat the motion.

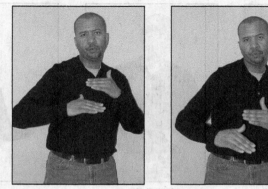

SNOWBOARDING

Move hands down as if sliding down a mountain.

SOCCER

Repeat the motion; a singular motion is KICK.

SWIMMING

*Repeat the motion; this sign looks as if you're swimming the
breaststroke.*

TENNIS

Motion as if swinging a tennis racket back and forth.

'TRACK

This is also the sign for COMPETE and RACE.

VOLLEYBALL

Some use a slightly different variation on this, such as flicking the middle fingers with the other fingers outstretched.

WRESTLING

COACH   TRACK   PLAYER

This is one of several varia-
tions; it is similar to BOSS.
Other ways include signing
MANAGER or finger-
spelling the word.

REFEREE   REFEREE

This is one of several varia-   *This is one of several variations.*
tions; this uses the BENT-V
handshape.

TOURNAMENT

Move hands in opposing directions.

GAME

This is also the sign for MATCH, MEET, and so on.

ACTIONS AND PLAYS

Equally important to sports signs is describing the plays or actions taken in a game. How you pass a ball in football is different from how you pass a ball in basketball or soccer.

Baseball

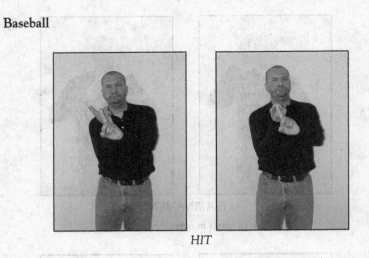

HIT

You can certainly use the sign for BASEBALL to show a hit, but this is more specific and shows that a ball was actually hit.

STRIKE

Bring the K toward the other hand.

THROW

CATCH

HOMERUN

Although this is fingerspelled H-R, there are nonmanual signals that accompany this word.

FOUL

Flick the index finger over your ear. Another way to sign this is to sign DIRTY; both signs are acceptable for all sports.

Basketball

PASS

SHOOT

DRIBBLE
Repeat the motion, as if dribbling a ball.

REBOUND

SLAM DUNK

POINT (game points)
Repeat the motion.

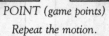

Football

PASS

Move hand as if throwing a football.

CATCH

FUMBLE

KICK   TOUCHDOWN

Although this is an actual
sign, most deaf athletes use
the next version.

TOUCHDOWN (TOUCH + T-D)

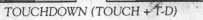

RANKINGS, SCORES, AND RECORDS

What are sports without rankings? In this section you learn how to boast about your team's wins or bemoan its losses.

WIN

LOSE

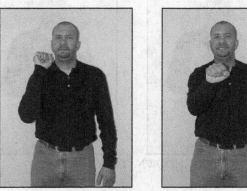

BEAT (We beat them 10–9.)

BEAT (They beat us easily.)

In sports, there is a specific way to state what rank a team has placed. I've already shown you the sign for CHAMPION in an earlier hour, so I'll show you the signs for first place and lower.

FIRST PLACE

EIGHTH PLACE

Note that this style of indicating placement can only be done for first through ninth place. Anything lower than ninth would be signed as TEN PLACE.

How you sign scores or records is also particular in ASL. Establishing spatial relationships, as discussed in Hour 7 (with the example of GIVE), is again a factor. For example, if your team has won a game 7–4, it will be signed as:

7   4

The winning number is usually signed first at the chest (to indicate that "my team won"), then the losing number. The signer starts at his chest, then moves into the space in front of his chest to indicate the other team's score. If your team is the losing team, the directionality shifts as shown in the following figures.

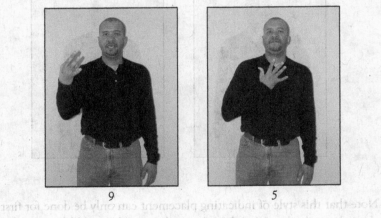

9   5

Notice how the directionality of the numbering changes for the losing score. If you're watching two teams that you aren't affiliated with, you will name the winning team, then name the score.

10   3

This indicates the winning   *This indicates the losing*
team, which is shown on   *team, shown on the opposite*
one side.   *side.*

This directionality is similar to how you say records.

Say a team has a losing record of 0–8:

0-8

Of course, if it's a winning record, the higher number will be
signed first.

Two other aspects of sports are important: stating heights and stating jersey numbers.

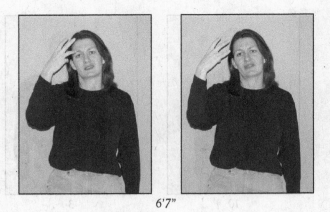

6'7"

The signer will show height by signing the number at a higher point, and the number will be turned inward (cardinal).

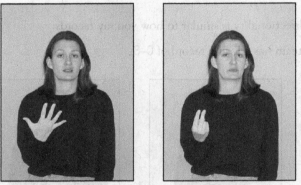

5'2"

The signer now signs at a lower point, since the person is short.

And if trying to say a person's jersey number?

3

Note how the signer puts the number *on* the jersey.

HANDS-ON PRACTICE

Here are two great activities you can do to get a head start on signing about sports events:

- Pick up a copy of a newspaper or sports magazine, and describe the various photographs in the publication. Include classifiers, descriptors, and actions. For instance, if you see a photograph of a slam dunk, describe how the basketball player looks as he dunks the ball; describe the other players around him; and describe how the crowd looks on.

- Look at the scoreboard or rankings in the sports section. Sign the different scores and numbers listed.

HOUR'S UP!

Here's a quiz to help you review some of the facts and ideas presented during this hour. (You can find the correct answers in Appendix A.)

1. What is the signer saying?

a. Cleveland won four games.

b. Chicago won four games.

c. Cleveland won ten games.

d. Chicago won ten games.

2. Who came up with the signals used by umpires today in baseball?

a. Dummy Hoy

b. Dummy Taylor

c. Richard Sipek

d. Curtis Pride

3. What is the signer saying?

a. I won $200.

b. I bowled a 200.

c. I won $300.

d. I bowled a 300.

4. Which sport is the signer referring to?

    a. Basketball

    b. Football

    c. Soccer

    d. Volleyball

5. Where was the football huddle invented?

    a. National Technical Institute for the Deaf

    b. Illinois School for the Deaf

    c. Gallaudet University

    d. American School for the Deaf

6. What was the final score?

a. 8–0

b. 0–8

c. 9–0

d. 0–9

7. What ranking did the team achieve?

a. 4th

b. 6th

c. 7th

d. 9th

8. What is the signer saying?

a. San Antonio lost the championship.

b. San Antonio won the championship.

c. Milwaukee lost the championship.

d. Milwaukee won the championship.

9. How did Boston fare?

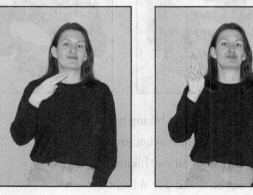

a. Boston won, thanks to a homerun.

b. Boston won, thanks to a strikeout.

c. Boston lost, thanks to a homerun.

d. Boston lost, thanks to a strikeout.

10. What is the signer saying?

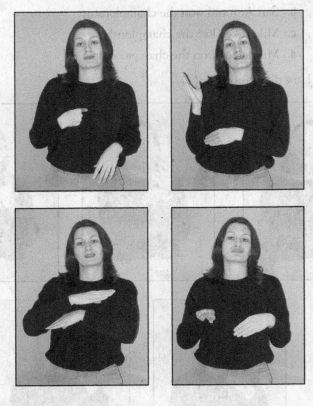

a. I went on a short hiking trip.

b. I went on a short skiing trip.

c. I went on an all-day hiking trip.

d. I went on an all-day skiing trip.

VOCABULARY LIST

Here's a summary of the signs you've learned in this hour:

BASEBALL	BASKETBALL
BEAT	BOWLING
CAMPING	CATCH
COACH	DRIBBLE
FOOTBALL	FOUL

QUIZ

FUMBLE	GAME
GOLF	HEIGHTS
HIKING	HIT
HOCKEY	HOMERUN
KICK	LOSE
PASS	PLAYER
POINT	RANKINGS
REBOUND	REFEREE
RUNNING	SHOOT
SKIING	SLAM DUNK
SNOWBOARDING	SOCCER
STRIKE	SWIMMING
TENNIS	THROW
TOUCHDOWN	TOURNAMENT
TRACK	VOLLEYBALL
WIN	WRESTLING

RECAP

In this hour, you learned about the importance of sports to the Deaf community. You also learned different signs for sports and actions/plays. In the next hour, I'll wrap up the lessons in this book and you'll learn about where to go next.

HOUR 24

What Next?

LESSON PLAN:

In this hour, we'll talk about ...

- ASL classes.
- Resources in your area.
- Recommended reading.

Y ou've taken a brief yet intense voyage into the fascinating world of ASL and Deaf culture, and hopefully you've learned a few signs that will help with ASL conversations.

Now what?

Good question. Some of the most common frustrations that ASL students experience are: "I don't know where to go; I can't seem to find any place where I can practice sign language." Or "I don't know of any books or videotapes that are good; most of them are written by hearing people or inexperienced signers." That's why we've elected to make this hour an hour of information and resources, rather than an ASL lesson. It might be the most valuable lesson of this book.

ASL CLASSES

Within the Deaf community, it is about who you know and where you go. As mentioned earlier in the book, you'll be accepted into the community somewhat better if you have a reason to be in the community; most often if you have a friend or co-worker (or relative) who is deaf or uses ASL, then you'll have a better reason for your interest in the community. So, it's a good idea to meet deaf people—besides, they're the ones who will teach you the actual language and culture.

First, if you aren't already enrolled in an ASL class, then it's a good idea to consider going that avenue. There's nothing like learning ASL from actual ASL users, especially deaf teachers. Good places to start are local colleges or local deaf organizations.

There are several important factors to consider when you're making your decision of which ASL class to take. A quick checklist that might help:

- Who are the people teaching? Are they ASLTA-certified or native signers?
- What is the philosophy of the program or organization offering the ASL class?
- What curriculum do they use? Do they teach ASL or other communication methods (such as contact sign language)?
- Are deaf people in any way involved with the ASL class?
- Do graduates or students who have taken the class recommend it? Do deaf people recommend the class?

A good way to learn more about ASL teaching standards is to contact ASLTA. The American Sign Language Teachers Association is an organization that certifies ASL teachers at varying levels. There are chapters in many states, and a biannual conference is held. The website also has posted the organization's guidelines on what to look for in an ASL teacher. For more information on teaching standards and certification, visit www.aslta.org.

A variety of helpful CDs, videotapes, and DVDs are on the market today to assist you in your ASL learning. One such videotape series that is popular among ASL students is the Bravo ASL Curriculum (available through Sign Enhancers at www.signenhancers.com), which consists of 15 videotapes and a 350-page student workbook in addition to activities. However, the price is a bit steep, so you may want to buy it one videotape at a time, or check your ASL program's language lab to see if they have it available for loan or viewing. The series offers excellent, easy-to-learn ASL lessons that are goofy yet educational at a pace that appeals to most ASL students. The signers involved are deaf.

As is true for this book, those CDs or DVDs and videotapes should be used only as tools for learning the language, rather than as an actual course or method. It's also important to check to see if deaf ASL users were directly involved in the development of these resources.

Resources in Your Area

Some of you might live in areas where there are a few or no immediate resources like those found in the big cities. Worry not. There are deaf organizations everywhere in America, and chances are there's a deaf organization or club near you. The Internet is one of the best options in trying to find local resources. Your deaf friends or co-workers (if you have any) also probably know where the local gatherings and/or events are; so ask them. However, it has always been a fact of the Deaf community that many deaf people will gladly drive long distances to attend events. This is less true nowadays with the Internet, but in the old days, it wasn't unusual for deaf people to drive a hundred miles just to gather with other deaf people. Although it's highly unlikely you'll need to drive a hundred miles, don't be surprised if you have to drive 30 to 45 miles for an event.

A great spot to visit is the state school for the deaf, if one exists in your state (in some states, there are more than two, such as California and New York). It might be some distance from where you are, but it will be well worth the time and trip. Many deaf schools offer tours of their campuses as long as you contact them in advance, and some have museums or alumni rooms that offer a wealth of history.

These schools also often host high school tournaments or games that many deaf people—both local and from other states—attend. These events are a great way to meet deaf adults and to see an actual community gathering. Gallaudet University's Clerc Center website provides a comprehensive list of schools for the deaf—both residential and charter programs—at clerccenter.gallaudet.edu/InfoToGo/schools-usa.html.

Yet another good resource is your state commission for the Deaf/Hard of Hearing, although not all states have one. These commissions are governmental agencies at the state level that work to provide legislative advocacy with other state agencies, and provide training, education, and consultation in the state (although a majority of state commissions do not provide direct services). Many of the state commissioners are deaf themselves, and many of the staffers are also deaf. These commissions have information referral coordinators who can provide you with the exact information you need, or with specific details on gatherings and/or events in your area. To find out if there is a commission in your state, check the comprehensive list at www.mcdhh.state.mo.us/Links/State_Commissions.htm.

For families of deaf children, there are plenty of resources. To begin with, parents might want to contact the American Society for Deaf Children. The organization offers networking and different services, and can most certainly help you find resources in your area. They can be visited at www.deafchildren.org or called toll-free at 1-800-942-ASDC.

After you make or find a contact, the domino effect will take over from there. You'll be led to another resource, and pretty soon, you'll wonder how you could ever have missed these gatherings or people before. We've also listed a few national organizations and other resources in the appendix. These organizations' websites have information on chapters in your state, along with contact information.

COMMUNITY EVENTS

Attending community events is often required by ASL teachers, and this is with good reason. Even if you aren't in an ASL class or your teacher doesn't require you to attend these events, do try to go to some events. It's a great way to meet people, practice your signing skills and pick up on new signs, and learn about Deaf culture and the various people involved with the Deaf community.

A popular activity among both deaf and hearing people is going to the theatre. The National Theatre of the Deaf—yet another organization with a rich history—does national tours with both deaf and hearing actors. The award-winning NTD also offers workshops and summer camps for both deaf and hearing actors. To find out if the NTD will be touring in your area soon, check their schedule at www.ntd.org. An excellent book about the NTD is *Pictures in the Air: The Story of the National Theatre of the Deaf* by Dr. Stephen C. Baldwin.

There are many other deaf theatre groups or performers, such as award-winning Deaf West Theatre in California, Cleveland SignStage in Ohio, and local theatre groups. Gallaudet University has an outstanding theatre arts department that puts on quality performances open to the public. Other performing groups include the Wild Zappers, a dance group from Washington, D.C.; TOYS Theatre, a group of deaf Russian performers; and many individual performers.

Many cities also offer interpreted theatre performances, where high-caliber productions are interpreted at well-known theatres. To find these performances, try contacting local interpreting agencies and finding out if they have calendars or listings of such events.

Another popular community event are "deaf expos." There are three companies that offer exposition shows or trade shows focusing entirely on products and services for deaf and hard of hearing people. These shows often attract thousands of attendees and hundreds of exhibitors. Skits, presentations, and workshops are also provided at these expos. Deaf Expo has a website at www.deafexpo.com; DeafWorldWide can be viewed at www.deafworldwide. com; and the third one is DeafBuy, which is advertised at www.deafbuy.com.

If you'd like to experience complete immersion in ASL, try attending a Silent Weekend or ASL Camp. Often sponsored by interpreter preparation programs or state chapters of the RID, these events usually take place over the weekend at a camp retreat location. Participants, upon arrival, are immediately asked to turn off their voices (talking is a no-no when using ASL), and communicate only in ASL for the entire duration of the weekend. Often challenging for people who are accustomed to using voice 24 hours a day, it is a great experience for signers. If they do use their voices and are caught, they usually have to endure some sort of punishment, such as wearing a silly hat, until the next person is caught using voice. The weekend consists of activities and workshops completely focused on ASL, for everyone from beginning signers (or nonsigners) to experienced signers/ interpreters. This is a highly recommended event for ASL signers of all levels.

Another ASL immersion program is the one offered by Gallaudet University's ASL program. The program lasts two weeks and is taught by experienced ASL teachers. These immersion environments are a good way to get some true hands-on practice with ASL with both hearing and deaf people, and they're also great for working with diverse levels and types of ASL skills. Contact either your state RID chapter or Gallaudet University for information on these events.

Sporting events are an excellent gathering spot. Although I've covered this in Hour 23, they are still worth a mention here. There are events for every sport or recreation event possible, from the common sports (basketball, bowling, and softball) to the unique ones (disc golf, flag football, and skydiving). A search on the Internet will turn up quite a few websites, but the best source is USADSF, which provides links to individual sports organizations, or the local and regional deaf club/athletic organizations. There are also regional tournaments in addition to local and national competitions, which can be found at USADSF's website.

The World Recreation Association for the Deaf is another organization that offers international recreational events. Its site is at www.wrad.org.

A comprehensive site that offers individual links to sports or recreation events not affiliated with USADSF is the About.com site. There is a category devoted to deaf topics, and the list of sports and recreation links is found at deafness.about.com/cs/recreation.

Let's not forget captioned movies, which I mentioned earlier in the book. These movies are a great way for families with deaf people, or hearing and deaf friends, to enjoy movies together. There are movies that have open captions—that is, the captions appear on the screen itself—and are shown at specific times and locations. Then there are movie theaters that offer rearview captioning (RVC, although it is also known as rear window captioning or RWC), where one uses an odd-looking device to read captions. Theaters offering rearview captioning often have movies available at any time, but it's always a good idea to check out show times and locations. For open-captioned movie listings, check www.tripod.org, and for RVC movies, go to the website at ncam.wgbh.org/mopix.

These are only some of the events or gatherings you might want to participate in. There are gatherings of deaf people for every reason possible: scrapbooking, quilting, hunting, financial gatherings, workshops, and many more. Again, after you make a contact, you'll immediately develop more contacts and find more information soon after that.

RECOMMENDED READING

If you're still hungering for more information on Deaf culture, ASL, and other deaf-related topics, there's plenty of reading available for you. Several books that are popular with ASL students are in the following list. Be sure to check also your local library or visit one of the vendors listed in Appendix C to check out more resources.

- A *Journey Into the Deaf-World* by Harlan Lane, Robert Hoffmeister, and Ben Bahan. (Dawn Sign Press, 1996)
  This is an insightful look into the Deaf-World. Bahan is a Deaf (he'd kill me if I described him with a small d) person with Deaf parents; Hoffmeister is a CODA; and Lane is a hearing person who has written numerous books about Deaf culture and the Deaf community. A wonderful mixture of these three people's viewpoints, the book gives an

in-depth look at Deaf culture and the people of the community, because this book *is* about the culturally Deaf community as opposed to the "general" deaf community. It also discusses signed language, technology, and provides many examples from deaf people's lives.

- *For Hearing People Only (Second Edition)* by Matthew S. Moore and Linda Levitan. (Deaf Life Press, 1993)

  This is a book in question-and-answer format; questions often asked by hearing people about deaf people or ASL are answered in an honest, easy-to-read style. This book is a requirement for anyone new to the community and a good read for people familiar with the community.

- *Deaf Heritage: A Narrative History of Deaf America* by Jack Gannon. (National Association of the Deaf, 1981)

  This is an encyclopedia of sorts that lists achievements, milestones, and noteworthy deaf individuals. It also provides a glimpse into the setbacks within the Deaf community, including the Milan Conference of 1880 and legislation that reduced rights. Although it is in need of an update, *Deaf Heritage* is a must-have in anybody's library.

- *Deaf World: A Historical Reader and Primary Sourcebook* by Lois Bragg (editor). (New York University Press, 2001)

  The book contains various essays, speeches, and writings by a variety of individuals within the Deaf community, both deaf and hearing from the past and present. A variety of topics is also discussed: genetics, intermarriage, education, ethics, language, biases, and portrayal of deaf people in the media. It compiles an excellent mosaic of writings that provide a good glimpse into the "Deaf World."

- *Great Deaf Americans (Second Edition)* by Matthew S. Moore and Robert F. Panara. (Deaf Life Press, 1996)

  This book has 77 biographical profiles of deaf people working in a variety of fields, and offers a good sense of the diversity of deaf identities, including culturally Deaf, oral, and late-deafened Americans.

Many ASL and interpreter preparation programs at colleges have labs or libraries with plenty of reading materials, in addition to videotapes, on ASL and Deaf culture. It's a good idea to read books not only about Deaf culture, but also the varying aspects of the Deaf community—such as late-deafened adults, parents of deaf children, and children of deaf adults.

Some deaf-owned or deaf-run vendors who sell these books and other deaf-related materials are listed in the appendixes.

THE REST OF THE JOURNEY

As mentioned early in the book, the only way you'll become fluent at American Sign Language is if you practice your skills, socialize with deaf people, and constantly work at becoming fluent. It's not an easy language to learn, but it's not impossible, either. ASL is such a fun, complicated language—and the culture is rich, full of experiences and interesting people.

Whatever your reasons for learning ASL, you'll meet diverse types of people from all walks of life in the Deaf community. A majority of them will be thrilled to welcome you into their community, even as close-knit as they might be. You'll also encounter cultural norms that might seem awkward, even strange, to you—and opinions that you might not always agree with. But even better, you'll also encounter amazing cultural experiences.

You might be rejected at times, or feel awkward about trying to enter such a close-knit community that uses a language you're not fluent at yet. The feelings you experience might be discouraging, and you might feel you aren't welcome or shouldn't continue to learn the language.

You'll also meet such diverse people that have differing perspectives on ASL, Deaf culture, issues, and socializing. It does get confusing at times. Who do you trust? Who's right? Who's wrong? Just like any other community, opinions, experiences, and values are very different from person to person.

The most important things you can do as a novice signer are to be open-minded, be upfront, embrace your signing skills (even if you feel they're poor), be respectful of the culture and language, and be respectful of the individual.

With these traits, and an understanding of ASL, you'll be well on your way in becoming part of a new community.

PART VI
Appendixes

PART VI

Appendixes

APPENDIX A
Answer Key

How well did you do in the quizzes? This appendix provides the answer key for the quizzes in Hour 1 through 23.

HOUR 1

1. b, d	**2.** a	**3.** c
4. b, c	**5.** c	**6.** b
7. False	**8.** c	**9.** a
10. True		

HOUR 2

1. b	**2.** d	**3.** a
4. b	**5.** a, b, c	**6.** a, b, c, d
7. False	**8.** b	**9.** b, c
10. c		

HOUR 3

1. b	**2.** False	**3.** c
4. False	**5.** a, b, c	**6.** a
7. d	**8.** True	**9.** a
10. b		

Hour 4

1. d	**2.** a	**3.** d
4. c	**5.** a, d	**6.** b
7. True	**8.** c	**9.** a
10. b		

Hour 5

1. False	**2.** a, c	**3.** b
4. c	**5.** d	

Hour 6

1. c	**2.** a	**3.** a, c
4. b	**5.** c	

Hour 7

1. True	**2.** b	**3.** d
4. b	**5.** c	**6.** c
7. True	**8.** d	**9.** a
10. b, c, d		

Hour 8

1. True	**2.** c	**3.** b
4. c	**5.** c	**6.** d
7. b	**8.** True	**9.** d
10. False		

Hour 9

1. c	**2.** True	**3.** d
4. a	**5.** False	**6.** c
7. c	**8.** False	**9.** d
10. a, b, d		

Hour 10

1. b	**2.** False	**3.** a, c, d
4. d	**5.** d	**6.** False
7. c	**8.** a	**9.** b, c, d
10. b		

Hour 11

1. a, b, c	**2.** a, c	**3.** True
4. c	**5.** c	**6.** a
7. b	**8.** d	**9.** a, b
10. False		

Hour 12

1. c	**2.** b	**3.** False
4. d	**5.** True	**6.** c
7. d	**8.** a	**9.** d
10. c		

Hour 13

1. c	**2.** True	**3.** True
4. f	**5.** c	**6.** g
7. e	**8.** a	**9.** d
10. b		

Hour 14

1. a, b, d	**2.** c, d	**3.** a
4. a, b, d	**5.** d	**6.** d
7. a	**8.** d	**9.** c
10. b		

Hour 15

1. a	2. True	3. b
4. d	5. c	6. c
7. d	8. a	9. c
10. a		

Hour 16

1. b	2. False	3. True
4. a	5. d	6. d
7. c	8. False	9. a
10. a		

Hour 17

1. True	2. c	3. False
4. b	5. b	6. d
7. a	8. d	9. b
10. d		

Hour 18

1. a	2. c	3. a, b, d
4. False	5. d	6. c
7. a	8. c	9. b
10. a		

Hour 19

SUNDAY	MONDAY	TUESDAY	WEDNESDAY	THURSDAY	FRIDAY	SATURDAY
	Daily: School	1	2	3 Bought a new car	4	5
6	7	8	Went to bed at 9 p.m.	10 Got up at 7 a.m.	11 Go to father's house	12 Dog gets bath
13	14 4:00 Dentist	15 Meet uncle	16 12:00: Meet friend	17	18	19
20	21	22	23	24 Son comes home!	25	26
27	28	29	30			

Hour 20

1. c   2. b   3. b

4. a   5. c   6. d

7. b   8. d   9. a

10. c

Hour 21

1. a   2. c   3. a

4. d   5. a   6. c

7. a   8. b   9. d

10. c

Hour 22

1. c   2. True   3. b

4. c   5. a, b, c, d   6. a

7. b   8. c   9. a

10. d

Hour 23

1. d   2. a   3. b

4. a   5. c   6. c

7. b   8. c   9. a

10. c

APPENDIX B

Organizations for Deaf People

Hundreds of organizations and agencies serve the deaf community; I can't list them all here. But I'll certainly list the major ones. However, a compilation of all the national organizations relating to deaf issues can be found at clerccenter.gallaudet.edu/InfoToGo/184.html.

American Association of the Deaf-Blind
814 Thayer Ave., Suite 302
Silver Spring, MD 20910-4500
(301) 495-4402 TTY
(301) 495-4403 Voice
(301) 495-4404 Fax
www.aadb.org

American Sign Language Teachers Association
814 Thayer Ave.
Silver Spring, MD 20910-4500
www.aslta.org

American Society for Deaf Children
P.O. Box 3355
Gettysburg, PA 17325
1-800-942-2732 TTY/Voice
(717) 334-7922 TTY/Voice
(717) 334-8808 Fax
www.deafchildren.org

Association of Late-Deafened Adults, Inc.
1131 Lake St. #204
Oak Park, IL 60301
(708) 358-0135 TTY
1-877-907-1738 FAX
www.alda.org

National Association of the Deaf
814 Thayer Ave.
Silver Spring, MD 20910-4500
(301) 587-1789 TTY
(301) 587-1788 Voice
(301) 587-1791 FAX
www.nad.org

National Theatre of the Deaf
55 Van Dyke Ave., Suite 312
Hartford, CT 06106
1-800-300-5179 TTY/Voice
(860) 724-5179 TTY/Voice
(860) 550-7974 Fax
www.ntd.org

Registry of Interpreters for the Deaf
333 Commerce St.
Alexandria, VA 22314
(703) 838-0459 TTY
(703) 838-0030 Voice
(703) 838-0454 Fax
www.rid.org

Self Help for Hard of Hearing People
7910 Woodmont Ave., Suite 1200
Bethesa, MD 20814
(301) 657-2249 TTY
(301) 657-2248 Voice
(301) 913-9413 Fax
www.shhh.org

Telecommunications for the Deaf, Inc.
8630 Fenton St., Suite 604
Silver Spring, MD 20910-3803
(301) 589-3006 TTY
(301) 589-3786 Voice
(301) 589-3797 Fax
www.tdi-online.org

USA Deaf Sports Federation
102 North Krohn Place
Sioux Falls, SD 57103-1800
(605) 367-5761 TTY
(605) 367-5760 Voice
(605) 367-5958 Fax
(866) 273-3323 Toll-free TTY
1-800-642-6410 Toll-free Voice
www.usadsf.org

These schools also have resource centers or programs:

National Center on Deafness
California State University,
Northridge
18111 Nordhoff St.
Northridge, CA 91330-8267
(818) 677-2054 TTY/Voice
(818) 677-7192 Fax
ncod.csun.edu

Gallaudet University
800 Florida Ave., NE
Washington, DC 20002-3695
(202) 651-5000 TTY/Voice
www.gallaudet.edu

National Technical Institute for the Deaf
Lyndon Baines Johnson Building
52 Lomb Memorial Drive
Rochester, NY 14623-5604
(585) 475-6840 TTY/Voice
(585) 475-5623 Fax
www.ntid.edu

APPENDIX C

Where to Buy Books and Materials

Although there are numerous deaf-owned and deaf-run businesses, there's only enough space to list a few here. Listing these vendors does not demonstrate my support of any one vendor; the list is for informational purposes only.

AGO Publications
P.O. Box 7193
Salem, OR 97303
(503) 373-1413 TTY
(503) 409-8972 Voice
(503) 304-1961 Fax
www.agostore.com

Dawn Sign Press
6130 Nancy Ridge Dr.
San Diego, CA 92121-3223
1-800-549-5350 TTY/Voice
(858) 625-0600 TTY/Voice
(858) 625-2336 Fax
www.dawnsignpress.com

Deaf Life Press
c/o MSM Productions, Ltd.
P.O. Box 23380
Rochester, NY 14692-3380
(585) 442-6370 TTY
(585) 442-6371 Fax
www.deaflife.com

Gallaudet University Press
800 Florida Ave., NE
Washington, DC 20002-3695
(202) 651-5488 TTY/Voice
(202) 651-5489 Fax
gupress.gallaudet.edu

Hear-More
42 Executive Blvd.
Farmingdale, NY 11735
1-800-281-3555 TTY
1-800-881-4327 Voice
(631) 752-0689 Fax
www.hearmore.com

Harris Communications
15155 Technology Dr.
Eden Prairie, MN 55344-2277
1-800-825-9187 TTY
1-800-825-6758 Voice
(952) 906-1099 Fax
www.harriscomm.com

Pyram
10000 Indiana Ave., Suite 9
Riverside, CA 92503-5419
(928) 438-8620 FAX
www.pyram.com

APPENDIX D

Internet Resources

While there are hundreds of resources on the Internet, I've selected the ones that may be most helpful for your learning ASL and about Deaf culture. Many of these sites or lists have additional links and/or resources.

WEBSITES

American Sign Language Teachers Association
www.aslta.org

Cindy's ASL Page
www.aslinfo.com

Deafness/Hard of Hearing (by About.com)
deafness.about.com

Gallaudet University
www.gallaudet.edu

National Association of the Deaf
www.nad.org

National Technical Institute for the Deaf
www.ntid.edu

Registry of Interpreters for the Deaf
www.rid.org

MAILING LISTS

DeafDigest
Newsletter-type e-zine
www.deafdigest.com

Deaf-L
Discussion group
www.zak.co.il/deaf-info/old/administrative.html

DeafSportsZine
E-zine about deaf sports
www.deafsportszine.com

e-Success (by Real World Success)
E-zine containing success stories and inspirational anecdotes
www.realworldsuccess.com/e-success.html

The Tactile Mind Weekly
E-zine containing observations and articles on the deaf community.
The Tactile Mind is a deaf-run literary publication.
www.thetactilemind.com

USA-L News
News and newspaper articles about deaf-related topics
USA-L_News-subscribe@yahoogroups.com

The Yahoo! Groups website (groups.yahoo.com) also has hundreds of deaf-related mailing lists.

APPENDIX E

Bibliography

This appendix lists the books cited in this book.

Baker-Shenk, Charlotte, and Dennis Cokely. A Teacher's Resource Text on Grammar and Culture. Washington, D.C.: Gallaudet University Press, 1980.

Gallaudet, Edward Miner. *History of the College for the Deaf 1857–1907*. Washington, D.C.: Gallaudet University Press, 1983.

Gannon, Jack R. *Deaf Heritage: A Narrative History of Americia*. Silver Spring, MD: National Association of the Deaf, 1981.

Lane, Harlan, Robert Hoffmeister, and Ben Bahan. *A Journey into the DEAF-WORLD*. San Diego: DawnSignPress, 1996.

Van Cleve, John Vickrey, and Barry A. Crouch. *A Place of Their Own: Creating the Deaf Community in America*. Washington, D.C.: Gallaudet University Press, 1989.

Index

B

E

H

X–Y–Z